COMING OUT OF BONDAGE

GOD'S STRATEGIC PLANS FOR FINANCIAL BREAKTHROUGHS

Folake Hassan

The Righteous Publishing House

London UK

COMING OUT OF BONDAGE

ISBN: 978-0-9928684-3-7

Published by The Righteous Publishing House

Flat 7, 93 Villiers Road

Willesden. London NW2 5QB

Visit our website at www.theblessedchristian.co.uk

APPRECIATION

I give all praises to God Almighty, who chose me and qualified me to be a Christian. I thank God for empowered me to study His Word and for blessing me with His Wisdom. My sincere appreciation also goes to the men and women from every part of the world that God has used to minister His Words to bless me. I thank my children for their good attitude that have enabled me to walk a good walk in my journey as a Christian. I thank my parents for taking good care of me through my childhood and they still do today.

Table of Contents

INTRODUCTIONS

Coming out of bondage means coming out of poverty. It means coming out of lack. It means coming out of shame forever in The Name of Jesus Christ.

In The Bible, it was written that The Children of Israel found themselves in the Nation called Egypt where their taskmaster subjected them to the lifestyle of slavery, and God heard their groaning's and God promised to delivered them from the ugly situations they found themselves.

The Bible advices that we wrestle not against flesh and blood (Ephesians 6:12), coming out of bondage is not intended to condemn those that lives or are from the country called Egypt. God loves all humanity, He does not want anyone to perish, everyone that accepts Jesus Christ as their Lord and Saviour is saved, whatever their colour, gender, race or background. If you have prayed the prayer of salvation and confess Jesus Christ as your Lord and Saviour, you are saved.

Egypt according to the Bible expression was a geographical location where the Israelites found themselves several years ago before the birth of our Lord and Saviour Jesus Christ. The Israelites went through some years of hardship in the hand of their taskmasters, the Egyptians, but God eventually freed them.

1

GOD IS STILL ALIVE TODAY, HE IS NOT DEAD AND HE IS READY TO SAVE AND BRING HIS CHOSEN ONES OUT OF EVERY SITUATION THAT DOES NOT GLORIFY GOD.

The Lord promised the Israelites (All Christians) that He will bring them out of bondage. My prayer is that the Word of The Lord will come through and true for each and every one of us speedily in The Mighty Name of Jesus Christ.

Coming out of bondage does not necessarily mean leaving your geographical location and it may mean relocating to another geographical location where God is leading you, or it may mean God improving situations for you where you are. It may mean God empowering you to be able to do some simple task that seems impossible for you such as being able to pay your bills, keeping your environment clean, or working to earn a meaningful incomes. It may mean God empowering you to improve in your attitude towards God and man. It may mean God healing you from all forms of pain, shame or abuse, it may mean God giving you a financial breakthrough, and it may mean God setting you free from all forms of embarrassments, it may mean God empowering you to overcome some ugly situations.

Chapter 1

COVENANT WITH GOD

And God heard their sighing and groaning and [earnestly] remembered His covenant with Abraham, with Isaac, and with Jacob (Exodus 2:24)

Looking at all the instances we will go through in this book, we shall see that all the people God brought out of bondages into His Abundant, no ending blessings have covenant with God. Right from inception God has been having covenant with His people. Immediately God created the first man and the woman (Adam and Eve) He tried to have a covenant with them by giving them the code of conduct that will qualify them for the kind of abundant life He wishes for them to have (see Genesis 3) though the covenant was broken; but God immediately promised Adam and Eve that He will send them a Saviour (Genesis 3:13-15). Having covenant with God Almighty is a prerequisite for God to move on behalf of someone to fight their battles. God is no respecter of persons, God is prepared to deliver anyone from every forms of calamities.

He is prepared to deliver anyone out of every unpleasant situations. I pray that we will not have a cause to deny God in The Name of Jesus Christ and I pray that God will grant us the grace to keep our own part of the covenant with Him in The Name of Jesus Christ.

If you are a Christian (a born again child of God), I say congratulations to you, remember that being a Christian and confessing Jesus Christ as our Lord and Saviour is not an ordinary event, it is a covenant with The God Almighty which must not be broken, this qualifies each and every one of us to fully receive the blessings God promised us in His Words.

> Dwell in Me, and I will dwell in you. [Live in Me, and I will live in you.] Just as no branch can bear fruit of itself without abiding in (being vitally united to) the vine, neither can you bear fruit unless you abide in Me. I am the Vine; you are the branches. Whoever lives in Me and I in him bears much (abundant) fruit. However, apart from Me [cut off from vital union with Me] you can do nothing. If a person does not dwell in Me, he is thrown out like a [broken-off] branch, and withers; such branches are gathered up and thrown into the fire, and they are burned. If you live in Me [abide vitally united to Me] and My words remain in you and continue to live in your hearts, ask whatever you will, and it shall be done for you (John 15: 4-7)

If you would like to become a Christian, may I advise you to do so by pray the prayer at the back of this book (on the pages after chapter 10) this will make you to become a Christian and it qualifies you for all the promises of God in The Bible.

God delights in man, even when Adam and Eve made a mistake by breaking covenant with God, God made a cover and cover them immediately and He promised deliverance through their seed (Jesus Christ). Though Jesus Christ is our Mediator that does not give us the license to be going about getting ourselves involved in all kinds of covenant that is contrary to Christ. The result of breaking covenant with God is not always too pleasant, therefore it is better to be safe than sorry by making sure that our commitment to the cause of Christ is intact.

Prayer: Lord, I pray that you will empower us to be able to keep our own side of the covenant with you in The Name of Jesus Christ.

God is a Jealous God

The covenant God cherished is the one we make with Him, God wants to be the Number one in our lives, He want to be the only God. No matter where we go, no matter where we find ourselves. God does not want us to be involved in any forms of activities that is contrary to His Word in other to gain fame, power or wealth; but to know that wherever we find ourselves ONLY THE WILL OF GOD MUST BE DONE. God doesn't want to share His glory with anyone or any other gods, so, when you are thinking of a covenant or agreement with anyone concerning anything, be sure that your love for God is intact and that God is the number one in your life, because; in the day of trouble when men's strength may not seems to be enough, God will always be there for you.

> You shall have no other gods before or besides Me. You shall not make yourself any graven image [to worship it] or any likeness of anything that is in the heavens above, or that is in the earth beneath, or that is in the water under the earth; You shall not bow down yourself to them or serve them; for I the Lord your God am a jealous God, visiting the iniquity of the fathers upon the children to the third and fourth generation of those who hate Me. (Exodus 20:3-5)

The Israelites broke their covenant with God because they thought His plan for them was taking too long, they created for themselves golden images to worship and God promised to bring punishment on them but **Moses besought the Lord on their behalf by putting God into remembrance of His covenant with Abraham, Isaac and Jacob.** Because of the covenant God has with Abraham, God's wrath against the Children of Israel was pacified.

And the Lord said to Moses, I have seen this people, and behold, it is a stiff-necked people; now therefore let Me alone, that My wrath may burn hot against them and that I may destroy them; but I will make of you a great nation. But Moses besought the Lord his God, and said, Lord, why does Your wrath blaze hot against Your people, whom You have brought forth out of the land of Egypt with great power and a mighty hand? Why should the Egyptians say, for evil He brought them forth, to slay them in the mountains and consume them from the face of the earth? Turn from Your fierce wrath, and change Your mind concerning this evil against Your people. [Earnestly] remember Abraham, Isaac, and Israel, Your servants, to whom You swore by Your own self and said to them, I will multiply your seed as the stars of the heavens, and all this land that I have spoken of will I give to your seed, and they shall inherit it forever. Then the Lord turned from the evil which He had thought to do to His people. (Exodus 32: 9-14)

If there was no covenant between God and Abraham, only God knows what would have become the children of Israel when they sinned against God.

My Personal Testimony That God Is A Covenant Keeper

I was born into a family that believes in Islamic faith, but fortunately, I and my siblings have the opportunity of worshipping with the Christian denominations that surrounds our residence from as early as when I was just about four years old. We attended churches occasionally especially whenever they are having crusades and events. I could remember some occasions when we gathered with some churches during their various services as early as when I was seven years old. Though some of their activities then does not have much meanings to us then, but God gave us the grace to be in the atmosphere where Christians ministered and because of this grace, we developed a good level of faith right from childhood. I could remember an occasion when I and my stepbrother went to go and kneeled in front of a church gate to pray to God to grant us success in our examinations. Miraculously in the year 1979 God granted me the grace to become a full time member of the Anglican church, I got baptized and started receiving Holy communion. I was baptized by The Bishop of Ekiti diocese then (the bishop in charge of a state in the southern part of Nigeria) The Late Archbishop Abiodun Adetiloye.

In 1984 God led me to start worshipping with a new denomination popularly knowing as Cherubim and Seraphim (C & S) in Lagos Nigeria. A day came when God spoke to me through my Pastor (popularly called Daddy) He advised me to take my relationship with Jesus Christ a bit more serious by making Jesus Christ the only God I served and worshiped, he advised that if I can do that it shall be well with me. I thank God for empowering His people to believe, I thank God for the simple childlike faith he gave me by empowering me to accept the guidance of my Pastor then in the year 1984. In 1996 I had an encounter with God after some days of prayer and fasting, the encounter made me to recommit my life to Christ by becoming A Born Again Christian.

Most of the churches I attended before becoming a born again Christian in the year 1996 doesn't emphasises that accepting Christ means also studying the Word of God regularly, therefore, I was not aware that for me to be truly be strong and become the ordained woman of God He intended me to be, I must study my Bible on a daily basis, but the idea and the believes that anyone who accepted Christ as their Lord and Saviour shall not perished stayed with me. I held on to that simple truth that the Name of Jesus shall save me in the day of trouble because that was the point my pastor emphasised. Though we were not aware that we must study the Bible daily then nor rooted on the Word of God, the covenant with the Almighty God within me kept me and is still keeping me and will continue to keep me. Though I did not know many scriptures at all but within me I know that anyone that have a covenant with Jesus Christ is saved, so no matter what I went through or going through, I always believe that everything will be alright because whoever has confessed Jesus Christ as their Lord and Saviour is saved, it was like holding on to an anchor which we must not let go.

The Name of Jesus will work wonders for anyone provided you can hold on to it, provided you can have your absolute trust in it, this confirm the title of a book written by Kenneth and Gloria Copeland that "One Word from God can Change Your Prayer Life". **The Name of Jesus worked wonders for me in the night season of life and is still working wonders today.** The Name of Jesus cannot lose its power in the life of those that choose to believe in Him. Having a covenant with God in The Name of Jesus Christ is between you and God and you must try all you can to make sure that you do not waver or be drifted from it.

It does not matter where and when you whispered the prayer in your heart, provided you can hold on to the truth, help will find you miraculously in the day of trouble. The Light of God will find your dwelling places to bless you and to set you free from all evils. This type of unusual favour and blessings usually comes to those that will not compromise their faith in Christ Jesus Christ.

In the day of challenge and spiritual warfare, the Name of Jesus brought me helps from around the world, The Lord God sent me helps from His sanctuary to proved that He cannot break His covenant. The Lord God empowered people that do not really know me to stand to do my warfare. The Lord God proved Himself that He is the Allknown God (Omnipresent). He proved Himself that He is A Covenant Keeping God.

In 1996, 12 years after I rededicated my life and accepted Jesus Christ as my Lord and Saviour, I found myself in a spiritual battle, a spiritual challenge after some days of prayer and fasting. The good part of this testimony was the fact that miraculously God appointed souls, Ministers, Elders, Pastors to do my warfare. Some of them prayed, some fasted, some kept vigil in my flat and some posted magazine to me from the furthermost part of the world and I was delivered from evil, I was delivered from death. What I am trying to say is that if you have a covenant with God, it does not matter where you prayed or whispered the prayer of salvation. God will miraculously speak on your behalf, He will speak to someone somewhere to do good and you will become part of the beneficiary of God's Idea through someone. God can make institutions and government to change laws in your favour (Study the story of Esther in the Book of Esther) to see how God stepped into a situations to favour Esther and her family.

What I held on to in the day of trouble was and is the Name "Jesus" because that was what I was given as the only solution to man's problem, believing that whosoever believe in that name will not perish. I held on to the Name of Jesus and God sent people my way that helped and lead me into the path of righteousness in Christ, I held on to the Name of Jesus; satan could not do me any harm.

My faith in Christ, the seed of the Word planted by the man of God in 1984 that "Jesus Christ is the Only Way" kept me from death, the simple faith kept me from sickness and from all the evils that satan intended for me. The spiritual battle, the spiritual challenge; the spiritual encounter then catapult me into a NEWER LEVEL OF CHRISTIAN FAITH WHICH I PRACTICE TILL TODAY AND FOREVER by being born again, hearing and loving the Word of God. The Word of God proves itself, the word of God works for me and it is capable of working for anyone that choose to accept the simple faith that "Jesus Christ is The Lord"

The Name of Jesus Christ works wonders for me because of the men and women of God who dedicated themselves to the cause of Christ, who chose to teach others and helped to signpost souls to Jesus Christ as The Way and The Truth. To God be The Glory for His faithfulness to mankind.

Therefore, I recommend for the reader of this book to rededicate themselves to God by confessing Jesus Christ as their Lord and Saviour and choose not to have any other god besides Him.

God made a covenant with Abraham, it was the covenant of blessings

If there was no covenant between God and Abraham, Isaac and Jacob, only God knows what would have become of the Children of Israel in the wilderness. As a result of the covenant God made with Abraham, God delivered The Israelites out of troubles several times. God emphasises in several passages of the Bible that whosoever have a covenant with Him shall be saved.

> Because if you acknowledge and confess with your lips that Jesus is Lord and in your heart believe (adhere to, trust in, and rely on the truth) that God raised Him from the dead, you will be saved. For with the heart a person believes (adheres to, trusts in, and relies on Christ) and so is justified (declared righteous, acceptable to God), and with the mouth he confesses (declares openly and speaks out freely his faith) and confirms [his] salvation. The Scripture says, No man who believes in Him [who adheres to, relies on, and trusts in Him] will [ever] be put to shame or be disappointed. [No one] for there is no distinction between Jew and Greek. The same Lord is Lord over all [of us] and He generously bestows His riches upon all who call upon Him [in faith]. For everyone who calls upon the name of the Lord [invoking Him as Lord] will be saved. (Romans 10:9-13)

I am sure the Israelites have prayed that God should improve situations for them, for the Bible says that.

And the Lord said, I have surely seen the affliction of My people who are in Egypt, and have heard their cry because of their taskmasters and oppressors; for I know their sorrows and sufferings and trials.

God chose someone to be in charge of delivering the Israelites from their bondages, in the Bible time; the name of the person chosen then was Moses (see Exodus 3:1-8) God Promised that they will not go out of Egypt empty handed:

> And I will give this people favour and respect in the sight of the Egyptians; and it shall be that when you go, you shall not go empty-handed. But every woman shall [insistently] solicit of her neighbour and of her that may be residing at her house jewels and articles of silver and gold, and garments, which you shall put on your sons and daughters; and you shall strip the Egyptians [of belongings due to you]. (Exodus 3:21-22)

God Will Not Send Anyone Away Empty Handed

If you have been waiting on God for answers and blessings concerning any area of your life, I can assure you that you will not come out of the situation disappointed, you shall not reap shame.

<u>Instances from The Bible</u>

a. After the Israelites has been in Egypt for more than 400 years, God promised to lead them into The Land of Canaan (The Land of Promise) The land flowing with milk and honey, a better place; a better space. God promised that the Israelites will not go empty handed (Exodus 3: 21-22)

b. Jacob served Laban his Father-In-Law for several years based on an agreement, the household of Laban prospered because of Jacob's presence in the family, but a day came when Laban's sons started complaining thinking that Jacob has taken all that belongs to their father. In the midst of it all God visited Jacob, He gave him a battle plan and He told him to start getting himself ready to move:

> Jacob heard Laban's sons complaining, Jacob has taken away all that was our father's; he has

17

acquired all this wealth and honour from what belonged to our father. And Jacob noticed that Laban looked at him less favourably than before. Then the Lord said to Jacob, Return to the land of your fathers and to your people, and I will be with you. (Genesis 31:13)

The above scriptures is not to encourage anyone to start robbery or to start running away with other peoples properties, it is to encourage us to learn how to guide and protect that which belongs to us. We should not be wasteful, but to learn to manage our resources well, to be a good steward of God's resources.

c.   Jesus fed 5000 men, women and children not counted with five loaves and two fish. He did not send them away empty handed.

As Jesus landed, He saw a great crowd waiting, and He was moved with compassion for them, because they were like sheep without a shepherd; and He began to teach them many things. And when the day was already far gone, His disciples came to Him and said, this is a desolate and isolated place, and the hour is now late. Send the crowds away to go into the country and villages round about and buy themselves something to eat. But He replied to them, Give them something to eat yourselves.

And they said to Him, Shall we go and buy 200
denarii [about forty dollars] worth of bread and
give it to them to eat? And He said to them,
how many loaves do you have? Go and see. And
when they [had looked and] knew, they said,
Five [loaves] and two fish. Then He commanded
the people all to recline on the green grass by
companies. So they threw themselves down in
ranks of hundreds and fifties [with the regularity
of an arrangement of beds of herbs, looking like
so many garden plots]. And taking the five
loaves and two fish, He looked up to heaven
and, praising God, gave thanks and broke the
loaves and kept on giving them to the disciples
to set before the people; and He [also] divided
the two fish among [them] all. And they all ate
and were satisfied. (Mark 6:34-42)

Prayer
Whatever has humiliated you, thinking that there is no help
for you shall be put to shame in The Name of Jesus Christ.
Whatever has thought that there is no help for you shall be
put to shame in The Name of Jesus Christ. Whatever
thinks that you have reached your dead ends shall be
disappointed in The Name of Jesus Christ.

It pleases God that Jacob should change his geographical
location, hence, God answered his prayer, hence God

appeared to Jacob while he was still at Laban's house, God showed him what to do to move to the next level of his life. God will show individuals what they needs to do to move to a better level in their live. We may not all needs to change our geographical locations, but we must all desire the best out of life, we must not settle for below the average living lifestyle. If the government of some nations can set a minimum wage levels, I am sure God desired His Children to live above average, and for their lives to matter and to be more relevant, not to live below the minimum wage level.

God is still alive, He is not dead, keep praying and trust God for that good change you desire, you will hear God clearly and He will direct you as to what you need to do in The Name of Jesus Christ.

As for the children of Israel in the book of Exodus, God gave them a battle plan:

**God appointed A Leader for them

**The Leader intercede on their behalf

**God told them to solicit for helps meaning to do something to find out what are the resources within their reach, not begging for alms, but to find out the helps in places they can tapped into, God empowered them to start desiring the best. The Lord God silenced every wrong voices and every wrong desires and believes system that makes them thinks that they can never have the best God planned for them. God empowered them to be in charge of economics of Egypt, God revealed to them the hidden riches of the secret places.

**God favoured them.

In the story of Jacob, God showed him how he would not be at a loss, God has promised that blessing will not depart from Abraham and his descendants, because God will not fail in His promises, He showed Himself strong on behalf of Jacob by showing him how to save what belongs to him.

> And if the God of my father, the God of Abraham and the Dread [lest he should fall] and Fear [lest he offend] of Isaac, had not been with me, surely you would have sent me away now empty-handed. God has seen my affliction and humiliation and the [wearying] labour of my hands and rebuked you last night. (Genesis 31:42)

Laban saw definitely that God was with Jacob, so he made a covenant with him:

> So come now, let us make a covenant or league, you and I, and let it be for a witness between you and me. (Genesis 31:42)

Prayer

God will show Himself strong on our behalf for the whole world to see that the God we serve is Alive and not dead, and that God will truly reward those whose mind and thoughts stays on Him. I pray that The Lord God Himself will remove from us every unnecessary evils that may want to distract our focus from His Words in The Name of Jesus Christ. The Lord God will enlarge our coast and favoured us abundantly beyond our imaginations in The Name of Jesus Christ. We shall be the head and not tail, we shall be the lender and not the borrowers in The Name of Jesus Christ.

The Lord God will prove to all humanity that He can bless all souls provided they are all in His covenant. The Lord God will show all humanity that He can never be short of resources to bless humanity. Heaven have enough resources to bless this generation and the generations to come.

Chapter 2

FELLOWSHIP WITH GOD

> This is the history of the generations of Noah. Noah was a just and righteous man, blameless in his [evil] generation; Noah walked [in habitual fellowship] with God (Genesis 6:9)

Fellowship with God is not only in the church, we must choose to fellowship with God not only when we are in the church, we must make it our habit to listen to what God will say to us during our fellowship with other Christians in a place of worship and in our moments of personal study and worship. As much as we have the opportunity, we must set time apart and create room and environment for the Spirit of The Living God to dwell in us, to dwell among us and to speak to us.

Our homes, cars and our spaces must be turned into a good place of worship as we have the opportunity by choosing to listen to good quality praise and worship songs regularly, by choosing to sing songs of praise to The Father God, by choosing to study The Word of God. We must not be too busy or too tired to listen and study the Word of God, by so doing we will developed a good relationship with God. The Word of God will empower us to be able to hear God clearly and obey Him concerning all things.

Fellowship with God will empower us to hear God clearly and it will save us from known and unknown troubles. The Bible clearly advices us to study the Word of God regularly for ourselves and in other for it to develop us to the points of being able to teach others.

> Study and be eager and do your utmost to present yourself to God approved (tested by trial), a workman who has no cause to be ashamed, correctly analyzing and accurately dividing [rightly handling and skillfully teaching] the Word of Truth. (2 Timothy 2:15)

> You will guard him and keep him in perfect and constant peace whose mind [both its inclination and its character] is stayed on You, because he commits himself to You, leans on You, and hopes confidently in You. So trust in the Lord (commit yourself to Him, lean on Him, hope confidently in Him) forever; for the Lord God is an everlasting Rock [the Rock of Ages]. (Isaiah 26: 3-4)

> The way of the [consistently] righteous (those living in moral and spiritual rectitude in every area and relationship of their lives) is level and straight; You,

O [Lord], Who are upright, direct aright and make level the path of the [uncompromisingly] just and righteous. (Isaiah 26:7)

God approved and blessed some people in the Bible because of the trust God had in them that they are capable of teaching the members of their households His Words.

Being capable of teaching the member of our household the Word of God is very important to God and it is part of what will qualify us to inherit the blessings God promised us.

1. And Enoch walked [in habitual fellowship] with God (Genesis 5:24)

2. But Noah found grace (favour) in the eyes of the Lord. This is the history of the generations of Noah. Noah was a just and righteous man, blameless in his [evil] generation; Noah walked [in habitual fellowship] with God. (Genesis 6:8-9)

3. For I have known (chosen, acknowledged) him [as My own], so that he may teach_and command his children and the sons of his house after him to keep the way of the Lord and to do what is just and righteous, so that

the Lord may bring Abraham what He has promised him (Genesis 18:19)

4.   And there was also a prophetess, Anna, the daughter of Phanuel, of the tribe of Asher. She was very old, having lived with her husband seven years from her maidenhood. And as a widow even for eighty-four years. She did not go out from the temple enclosure, but was worshiping night and day with fasting and prayer. And she too came up at that same hour, **and she returned thanks to God** and talked of [Jesus] to all who were looking for the redemption (deliverance) of Jerusalem. (Luke 2:36-38)

5. And they steadfastly persevered, devoting themselves constantly to the instruction and fellowship of the apostles, to the breaking of bread [including the Lord's Supper] and prayers (Acts 2:42)

For some of us that may want to complain about our dedications to the cause of Christ, I hope the story of Prophetess Anna (Luke 2:36-38) will encourage us to be willing to be more committed to the cause of Christ, knowing that weeping may have been for a night, but joy is definitely coming in the Name of Jesus Christ.

We do not need to wait to become widow before we accept our responsibility of studying the Word of God, so as to prepare us to teach the members of our households, so as to make us to be created in Gods Image, to be Christlike in nature, manifesting God's counsels everywhere we go.

The Lord advices that we should teach our children the ways of the Lord, when we acquaint ourselves with the Word of God, healing; health; peace; celebrations shall be a daily and normal experiences in our society.

We should never allow anything to separate us from the knowledge of the Word of God, we should never allow anything to entice us away from The Word of God. No amount of fame or prosperity should be allowed to separate us and our children from the Word of God. And we should pray always for God to keep us at the centre of His will for us.

The Word of God must become our blueprints for all things, we must crave for it, and we must create time to study it and to teach our children.

> Hear, O Israel: the Lord our God is one Lord [the only Lord]. And you shall love the Lord your God with all your [mind and] heart and with your entire being and with all your might. And these words which I am commanding you this day shall be [first] in your [own] minds and hearts; [then] You shall whet and sharpen them so as to make them penetrate, and teach and impress them diligently

upon the [minds and] hearts of your children, and shall talk of them when you sit in your house and when you walk by the way, and when you lie down and when you rise up. And you shall bind them as a sign upon your hand, and they shall be as frontlets (forehead bands) between your eyes. And you shall write them upon the doorposts of your house and on your gates. (Deuteronomy 6:4-9)

Then beware lest you forget the Lord, Who brought you out of the land of Egypt, out of the house of bondage. You shall [reverently] fear the Lord your God and serve Him and swear by His name [and presence]. You shall not go after other gods, any of the gods of the peoples who are round about you (Deuteronomy 6:1214)

Freedom In Christ

The thief comes only in order to steal and kill and destroy. I came that they may have and enjoy life, and have it in abundance (to the full, till it overflows) (John 10:10)

The Joy of Being Created in God's Image through His Word That Dwells in Us is to allow the Word of God to dwell in us richly and then go and be a good witness of the faithfulness of God to mankind.

> And the curtain [of the Holy of Holies] of the temple was torn in two from top to bottom (Mark 15:38)

Mark 15:38 is a good reference of how the veil that separated us from communicating with God was torn immediately after the death of Jesus, before His death; only the high priest was allowed into God's presence (see Exodus 32: 9-14). The high priest was the one who usually intercede for the people, but according to Mark 15:38 the torn in the veil is an opening for the believers to start studying the Word of God and receive solutions from The Word of God for all things, it gives them the free access to communicate with The Father God especially through prayers; it is an opening for the believers to pray a faith based and the Word of God based prayers. As a Christian we must be well versed in the Word of God which is one of the prerequisite to be A Good Christian.

To God be the glory for the freedom purchased for us through the blood of Jesus Christ. To God be the glory for the Great Commission we have in Christ Jesus:

> And He said to them, Go into all the world and preach and publish openly the good news (the Gospel) to every creature [of the whole human race]. (Mark 16:15)

This freedom means that we can all choose to study The Word of God and find out:

God's will about all things, it means we do not need to live in the darkness any more. We do not need to feel guilty as well if God is trying to establish us on the solid foundation of His will.

The freedom means people will no longer be ignorant about anything, it means the living condition of the people will improve, the crime rate, crises rate, sickness and poverty rate will be reduced and eliminated completely in The Name of Jesus Christ, the truth of the Word of God will empower souls to know how to live right. GLORY BE TO GOD.

The Freedom means we will have sufficient number of knowledgeable Christian that can teach the Word of God, it means our productivity level will increase as we will be well illuminated to do things according to God's Will, the Bible says His plan for us is not grievous. It means there shall be no more weeping in our land, no more sorrow, everyone will know through the Word of God how to live right and thereby fulfilling the scripture in Revelation 21:4

> God will wipe away every tear from their eyes; and death shall be no more, neither shall there be anguish (sorrow and mourning) nor grief nor pain any more, for the old conditions and the former order of things have passed away (Revelation 21:4)

The Freedom means parents will be able to stay and be well equipped to take good care of their children and family by studying the Word of God. They will learn how to set their priorities right; there will be more orders in the family because the Word of God will be our foundations and the code of conducts for all things.

The Freedom means having enough strength, energy and encouragements to do some simple task such as being able to take a good employment, being able to be successful in our enterprises, having a sound mind for all things, it will empowers us to accept Godly responsibilities.

The Freedom in Christ means we will not become a burden to anyone, knowing the Word of God will strengthen us and save us from all evils, it will make us to be competent for all our God's given assignment.

The society is watching to see souls truly demonstrate that they are Christians through our attitudes, and we can only demonstrate the true character God desired from us by the levels of the knowledge of The Word of God in us.

Women Ministered To Jesus Christ

Our Freedom in Christ does not mean running away from our pastors and elders, it mean being matured, being prepared and being equipped to fellowship with them. It means being matured to accept responsibility, because studying the Word of God will illuminate us and prepared us for all things; it will convince us about what God requires from us about all things. FOR INSTANCE: the

Bible recorded that Mary Magdalene and Mary the mother of James were in the habit of accompanying and ministering to Jesus during His earthly assignment, they were among those who witnessed the miracle of the torn of the veil that separated them from The Holy of Holies (see Mark 15:40 – 41) Jesus paid the price for them to cross over from death to life, giving them the freedom to communicate with the Father and to pray to Him in The Name of Jesus Christ.

We read in several verses in the Bible that Jesus went from places to places teaching The Word of God and He wants His disciples to do the same. We will only teach what we know, hence the reason to allow The word of God to dwell in us richly, so that out of the abundance of our heart God's Wisdom will flow in The Name of Jesus Christ.

We must accept Our Freedom in Christ.

We may have been a baby Christian all our lives, maybe we have relied on other people around us to teach us the Word of God without any effort from our own side. A time should come when we should choose to create time, to set time apart to study The Word of God and find out what is God saying concerning the challenges we may face. And if God grant us the grace to study His Words, we must appreciate such opportunity, thank God for it and never take it for granted.

Studying the Word of God means studying from the Holy Bible directly, studying the trusted Christian Books, listening to the teachings from Christian Leaders. It means applying what we study to our situations by making good contributions towards the advancement of The Kingdom of God, it means sharing with our leaders what we learn from the Word of God.

More Instances from The Bible Where Maid Ministers to Their Masters

a. The maid of Naaman helped him by ushering him into his healing (2nd Kings 5: 1-19) Thank God for giving Naaman the wisdom to listen to the counsel of his maid.
b. Rhoda informed the Elders that God has answered their prayers concerning Peter. (Acts 12:12-15).

PRAYER

I pray that The Lord God will give us the grace to understand what God is trying to achieve in every stages of our Christian life. I hope this book will encourage someone to start studying the Word of God and start receiving the blessings The Lord has for them in The Name of Jesus Christ.

We don't retire from the Word of God, The word of God does not have an expiry date.

This Book of the Law shall not depart out of your mouth, but you shall meditate on it day and night, that you may observe and do according to all that is written in it. For then you shall make your way prosperous, and then you shall deal wisely and have good success (Joshua 1:8)

Chapter 3

OBEDIENCE

You shall serve the Lord your God; He shall bless your bread and water, and I will take sickness from your midst. None shall lose her young by miscarriage or be barren in your land; I will fulfil the number of your days (Exodus 23:25-26)

Doing the will of God will lead anyone out of every unpleasant situations. Doing the will of God will lead to blessings.

As soon as we are sure of the geographical location where God wants us to reside or even before we are sure of it, God delights in us to:

Pray regularly for our Nations

To pray regularly for our Leaders

To be involved in seeing the blessings of The Lord manifest in our land.

To pay our taxes regularly to our government

To pay our tithes and offerings to the churches that teaches us the Word of God

To serve voluntarily or paid in the household of faith

The Lord God advised the Israelites to apply The Holy Anointing Oil (the symbol of The Holy Spirit) to empowers them to make progress (Exodus 27:20, 37:29, 40:15)

***Also coming out of bondage may require a generous, liberal spirit: not to be too greedy for gains, not to be too anxious for gains (Exodus 13:3, Leviticus 19:23-25)

Coming out of bondage may require avoiding wastage, if anyone is obsessed with unhealthy eating habit, eating food without control and wasting some; then they should heed the Word of God and do something good by asking God to give them the Spirit of self-control(see Exodus 16, Leviticus 16:29, 1 Cor.6:13)

Prayer

You can pray and ask God to empower you to be able to hear and obey Him.

You can pray to God to empower you to be able to please Him and do His will at all times.

It pleases our Father when we do His will, for us to be truly out of unpleasant situations and start enjoying the blessings of The Lord without limits; we must acquaint ourselves with the Laws of God (The Word of God), our salvation though is complete in Christ, it delights God when we bear fruits and continue to bear more excellent fruits and the only way to bear fruits is by loving the law of God and living by its principles.

> Any branch in Me that does not bear fruit [that stops bearing] He cuts away (trims off, takes away); and He cleanses and repeatedly prunes every branch that continues to bear fruit, to make it bear more and richer and more excellent fruit (John 15:2)

Prayers for the Leaders and Our Nations

When the Leaders in a Nation makes good and Godly decisions, everyone is blessed and if everyone are blessed, then the joy of The Lord shall abound in the lives of His people. Good and Godly decisions by the Leaders in a Nation will result in good security, safety and peace for God's people. Hence God gave the assignment of praying for the Nations to the Christians. If the government is upon the shoulder of Jesus Christ, then the responsibilities is upon the churches and the Christians to do our best to keep the peace and the joy of our Nations. This put the Christians to be in charge of their Nations. This is a responsibility we must accept without anyone begging us to do so knowing that if it is well with our Nation, then we shall be the beneficiary of it.

1. For to us a Child is born, to us a Son is given; and the government shall be upon His shoulder, and His name shall be called Wonderful Counselor, Mighty God, Everlasting Father [of Eternity], Prince of Peace (Isaiah 9:6)

2. First of all, then, I admonish and urge that petitions, prayers, intercessions, and thanksgivings be offered on behalf of all men. For kings and all who are in positions of authority or high responsibility, that [outwardly] we may pass a quiet and undisturbed life [and inwardly] a peaceable one in all godliness and reverence and seriousness in every way. For such [praying] is good and right, and [it is] pleasing and acceptable to God our Saviour.
Who wishes all men to be saved and [increasingly] to perceive and recognize and discern and know precisely and correctly the [divine] Truth (1 Timothy 2:1-4)

3. And I sought a man among them who should build up the wall and stand in the gap before Me for the land, that I should not destroy it…….. (Ezekiel 22:30)

40

4. And He replied to them, this kind cannot be driven out by anything but prayer and fasting (Mark 9:29)

One of the commandments God gave was for us to love God and to love our neighbours, there is a saying that "it is not common to harm anyone we pray for" and "if we love anyone we will pray for them and wish them well". Prayer is a seed, since the law of the seed time and harvest shall never ceased, we tends to be a good beneficiary of the prayer we raised for someone, especially for our Nations. People have complained about things that are not right in our society often, instead of moaning and groaning about things that are not right, God commands us to remember to pray for God's Divine intervention in all things, we should pray for our leaders. What we make happens for others God is capable of making happens for us too, we should also pray for one another.

> ....pray [also] for one another, that you may be healed and restored [to a spiritual tone of mind and heart]. The earnest (heartfelt, continued) prayer of a righteous man makes tremendous power available [dynamic in its working] (James 5:16)

Prayer is not what we do only when we go to church, the Bible advices us to pray always without ceasing, which means that we should pray and wish someone well 24 hours every day. Not every prayer needs to be loud.

> Also [Jesus] told them a parable to the effect that they ought always to pray and not to turn coward (faint, lose heart, and give up) (Luke 18:1)

The Bible advices that we should make the ministry of a faith based prayers our ministry, it should become what we do on a regular voluntary basis.

> For physical training is of some value (useful for a little), but godliness (spiritual training) is useful and of value in everything and in every way, for it holds promise for the present life and also for the life which is to come (1 Timothy 4:8)

We thank God for delivering us from the wrong doctrines that says "only sick people needs prayers" thereby not making us to be fervent enough in the spirit as commanded by our Lord and Saviour, thereby causing the error of omission in Christians Prayer life. If we pray generally for our nations, then we shall not be omitting anyone from our prayers.

> Never lag in zeal and in earnest endeavour; be aglow and burning with the Spirit, serving the Lord (Romans 12:11) AMP.

> Not slothful in business; fervent in spirit; serving the Lord. Rejoicing in hope; patient in tribulation;

continuing instant in prayer (Romans 12:11-12) KJV

God commanded in His Words that men ought to pray and not to give up, prayer should be our lifetime practice, not what we do only when we see someone in dire needs of it, it should become our regular practice to pray at all times according to God's will, to teach our children to do the same and to trust God for all things.

> Also [Jesus] told them a parable to the effect that they ought always to pray and not to turn coward (faint, lose heart, and give up) (Luke 18:1)

For us to be able to do this effectively, we should ask God to pour more of His Spirit on us, to empower us to study His Words (the basis for our prayers) we should ask God to empower us to be able to truly make it our duty to pray and trust Him for our needs; to pray for everyone in positions of authority knowing that most of their decisions may influence our own progress. Therefore it is a good practise for all Christians to be aware of their responsibility to pray for all men, to pray for the salvation of souls and not to give up; to show our concern for the wellbeing of everyone in our society.

We Are To Pay Our Taxes Regularly to Our Government

The Bible advices us to owe no man anything but to love them, paying our taxes to our government is a way of empowering them to carry out some tasks on our behalf: to maintain the stability of our Nations, to provide some basic amenities for the citizens of our lands, it does not delight God whenever we decide not to pay the correct taxes, dodging to pay the taxes is a snare to any citizen. If the Bible and the Judiciary commands that we should be loyal to the governing authorities, then no one should remind us to pray to God to appoint for us The Leaders that has the referential fear of the Lord. We should have enough trust in our government believing that they will do the right things with the funds entrusted to them, our prayers should be strong enough to make the right Leaders to be in the positions of authority in our Nations. We must be willing to vote during the election periods trusting that God will truly place His Anointed Leaders in the positions of authority and those that needs training will accept the training. (See 1 Timothy 2: 1-4)

> Let every person be loyally subject to the governing (civil) authorities. For there is no authority except from God [by His permission, His sanction], and those that exist do so by God's appointment. Therefore he who resists and sets himself up against the authorities resists what God has

appointed and arranged [in divine order]. And those who resist will bring down judgment upon themselves [receiving the penalty due them]. For civil authorities are not a terror to [people of] good conduct, but to [those of] bad behaviour. Would you have no dread of him who is in authority? Then do what is right and you will receive his approval and commendation. For he is God's servant for your good. But if you do wrong, [you should dread him and] be afraid, for he does not bear and wear the sword for nothing. He is God's servant to execute His wrath (punishment, vengeance) on the wrongdoer. Therefore one must be subject, not only to avoid God's wrath and escape punishment, but also as a matter of principle and for the sake of conscience. For this same reason you pay taxes, for [the civil authorities] are official servants under God, devoting themselves to attending to this very service. Render to all men their dues. [Pay] taxes to whom taxes are due, revenue to whom revenue is due, respect to whom respect is due, and honour to whom honour is due. Keep out of debt and owe no man anything, except to love one another; for he who loves his neighbour [who practices loving others] has fulfilled the Law [relating to one's fellowmen, meeting all its requirements]. (Romans 13:18)

Therefore, the argument "we do not really know what they are doing with our taxes paid" should not happens if we are fully aware of the obligations placed on us as Christians to make it our duty to pray for our Nations, knowing that if we pray regularly,

God will appoint for us A Trustworthy Leaders who will manage our resources well. Also, we must not abstain from voting the right leaders into the positions of authorities.

No one as a Christian should lack the qualities and the Wisdoms necessary to truly manifest the Best God desired us to be, if anyone is not manifesting the blessings of The Lord as they should be, I will encourage them to give more attention to study The Word of God to receive revelations that will help them to be the best for God.

We Are To Pay Our Tithes and Offerings

God commands us to pay our tithes and offerings to the church that teaches us The Word of God and that helps us to take The Word of God to Nations on our behalf. Our tithes is the 10% of our income plus a bit of extra for offering which makes our giving to be more than 10% of our income. God commands us to do this regularly to help empowers the household of faith to stay in their calling, it will help them to devote more of their time to the things of God such as studying to hear the heartbeat of God for His churches, paying our tithes is a sure proof that we have conquered greed and it is a way of commanding God's blessings upon our lives. None of us will wants to do without having a regular income, we would not want our employers to pay us today and not pay us tomorrow, therefore as we wants men to do to us, we must be willing to do to others. Our tithes and offerings is not what we pay after paying our bills, we pay it first before spending on other necessities.

For the church of God to continue, for the Word of God to go round to Nations, for the Pastors and the Ministers to have time to study the Word of God and attends to the needs of their congregations, we must contribute to their needs. Apart from the fact that this is a good practise, God commands it:

> Bring all the tithes (the whole tenth of your income) into the storehouse, that there may be food in My house, and prove Me now by it, says the Lord of hosts, if I will not open the windows of heaven for you and pour you out a blessing, that there shall not be room enough to receive it. And I will rebuke the devourer [insects and plagues] for your sakes and he shall not destroy the fruits of your ground, neither shall your vine drop its fruit before the time in the field, says the Lord of hosts. (Malachi 3: 10-11)

Giving is a proof that we love someone, our giving to further the works of God is a proof that we truly love God and God promised that in return He will not allow sickness;

poverty and lack to come near us; He promised that premature death will not be our portion. Churches should teach their congregations more about the Wisdom of paying the correct amount of Tithes, by so doing, every unnecessary curses shall be broken from the Children of God in The Name of Jesus.

Serving is Part of What God Commands

Serving, especially in the household of faith has a good reward, serving should be done by following the procedure laid down by the church, it is a good practise after worshipping with a church for some time, to ask which department needs our helps; if the task they gave is something we are capable of delivering, then we should offer our voluntary or paid service. The place of serving is a place of blessings.

> You shall serve the Lord your God; He shall bless your bread and water, and I will take sickness from your midst. None shall lose her young by miscarriage or be barren in your land; I will fulfill the number of your days (Exodus 23:25-26)

Examples of People who served in The Bible

Moses served his father-in-law: "Now Moses kept the flock of Jethro his father-inlaw, the priest of Midian; and he led the flock to the back or west side of the wilderness and came to Horeb or Sinai, the mountain of God. **The Angel of the Lord appeared to him in a flame of fire** out of the midst of a bush; and he looked, and behold, the bush burned with fire, yet was not consumed" (Exodus 3:1-2)

Zechariah Served as A Priest: "In the days when Herod was king of Judea there was a certain priest whose name was Zachariah, of the daily service (the division) of Abia; and his wife was also a descendant of Aaron, and her name was Elizabeth. And they both were righteous in the sight of God, walking blamelessly in all the commandments and requirements of the Lord. But they had no child, for Elizabeth was barren; and both were far advanced in years. **Now while on duty, serving as priest before God in the order of his division.** As was the custom of the priesthood, it fell to him by lot to enter [the sanctuary of] the temple of the Lord and burn incense. And all the throng of people were praying outside [in the court] at the hour of incense [burning]. **And there appeared to him an angel of the Lord, standing at the right side of the altar of incense.** And when Zachariah saw him, he was troubled, and fear took possession of him. But the angel said to him, Do not be afraid, Zachariah, because your petition was heard, and your wife Elizabeth will bear you a son, and you must call his name John [God is favourable]. And you shall have joy and exultant delight, and many will rejoice over his birth" (Luke 1:5-14)

God Commands the Israelites to Take Communion

> The Lord said to Moses and Aaron in the land of Egypt, this month shall be to you the beginning of months, the first month of the year to you. Tell all the congregation of Israel, On the tenth day of this month they shall take every man a lamb or kid, according to [the size of] the family of which he is the father, a lamb or kid for each house. (Exodus 12:1-3)

Taking communion is our way of affirming, confirming and renewal of our faith in Christ Jesus. Jesus Christ commands that it should be done as a memorial to remind us of the price He paid on our behalf (Matthew 26:26-28, Mark 14:22-24, Luke 22:19-20, 1 Corinthians 11: 23-29)

Jesus took the communion with His disciples while He was alive with them which means that the communion took place while Jesus was and is alive. When we partake of the communion, what we are receiving is the life of Christ and all the blessings He purchased for us and not His dead body. What we are receiving is healing and not sickness, what we are receiving is freedom from fears and agitating passions and not bondage. What we are receiving is prosperities and not poverty.

Every Christian should be prepared to partake in the Holy Communion regularly, we must remember that God commanded this in the Chapter 12 of the book of Exodus, this should be done as a memorial and an ordinances from generation to generation to show of God's faithfulness to bring us out of every unpleasant situations. It is a form of seal to our prayers also and a form of agreement that God has answered our prayer.

> And this day shall be to you for a memorial. You shall keep it as a feast to the Lord throughout your generations, keep it as an ordinance forever (Exodus 12: 14)

We Must Plead the Blood of Jesus

Also by faith we must remember to cover ourselves with The Blood of Jesus regularly, especially if we want God to cleanse us from every form of filthiness.

God do not require from us any form of human sacrifice or the shed blood of animals or of that of humans, He want us by faith to accept the price paid on our behalf by our Lord and Saviour Jesus Christ several years ago and to affirm the sacrifice regularly. Once we plead the blood of Jesus or confess our acceptance of it that is sufficient for us to qualify for God's Divine Protection. For the life of every living creature is in the blood and we all need the blood of Jesus to run through our veins regularly because it is a Living Blood that has passed from death to life.

> As for the life of all flesh, the blood of it represents the life of it; therefore I said to the Israelites, You shall partake of the blood of no kind of flesh, for the life of all flesh is its blood. Whoever eats of it shall be cut off (Leviticus 17:14)

In the Old Testament of the Bible, the priest usually offered a bull or goats as a sacrifice to take away the sins of the Israelites, each time they falls into any kind of sin, the priest would make a sacrifice to annulled the sin, but we thank God for the price paid by Jesus Christ once and for all, we do not need to be carrying on with rituals killings of any human beings or that of the animals to atone for sins, Jesus paid it all. Pleading the blood of animals doesn't take away the sins completely but rather makes people to be more sins conscious and guilt conscious, anyone who has confessed Jesus Christ as their Lord and saviour is free from all sins and they should allow the blood of Jesus to cleanse them from all past sins, and they should keep away from anything that can contaminate their spirit.

> For by a single offering He has forever completely cleansed and perfected those who are consecrated and made holy. And also the Holy Spirit adds His

testimony to us [in confirmation of this]. For having said. This is the agreement (testament, covenant) that I will set up and conclude with them after those days, says the Lord: I will imprint My laws upon their hearts, and I will inscribe them on their minds (on their inmost thoughts and understanding) He then goes on to say, And their sins and their lawbreaking I will remember no more. Now where there is absolute remission (forgiveness and cancellation of the penalty) of these [sins and lawbreaking], there is no longer any offering made to atone for sin. Therefore, brethren, since we have full freedom and confidence to enter into the [Holy of] Holies [by the power and virtue] in the blood of Jesus, By this fresh (new) and living way which He initiated and dedicated and opened for us through the separating curtain (veil of the Holy of Holies), that is, through His flesh, And since we have [such] a great and wonderful and noble Priest [Who rules] over the house of God, Let us all come forward and draw near with true (honest and sincere) hearts in unqualified assurance and absolute conviction engendered by faith (by that leaning of the entire human personality on God in absolute trust and confidence in His power, wisdom, and goodness), having our hearts sprinkled and purified from a guilty (evil) conscience and our bodies cleansed with pure water (Hebrews 4: 14-22)

Because the blood of bulls and goats is powerless to take sins away
(Hebrews 10:4)

As Christians, we must remember to regularly cover ourselves with the Blood of Jesus. Pleading or covering ourselves with The Blood of Jesus is not what we do physically as in cutting our flesh, but by faith, this is what we should do through prayer and through our confession. Pleading the Blood of Jesus is acknowledging the price paid for us by our Lord and Saviour. Pleading the Blood of Jesus is acknowledging and accepting all the blessings attributed to God **(see my book "The Attributes of God" the Section that reminds us of The Names of God)**. Pleading The Blood of Jesus is a way of saying to forces everywhere that we bear the good mark of God's redemption power on our body, therefore no evil forces, no plagues; no calamities will come near our dwelling places in the Name of Jesus Christ (Psalm 91)

The Bible teaches that the life of every living soul is in the blood that runs through their veins (Leviticus 17:11) therefore we all needs the Living Blood of Jesus Christ to keep running through our veins to give us life without end.

As Christians, we must plead the Blood of Jesus on ourselves regularly by faith, meaning that no other blood of any kind will have power over us; meaning we are not equal to animals but a joint heirs with Jesus Christ. If anyone or any situations is trying to get us into an unknown covenant or agreement other than the truth of the

Word of God, it will not have an adverse effects on us, we shall walk away free from all evils in the Name of Jesus Christ because of the Blood of Jesus on us (see Psalm 91)

As Christians, we must not partake in cutting of our flesh or any other unnecessary shedding of bloods, we must not partake in any forms of rituals (Leviticus 17:14)

God wants us to be completely set aside for Him, He wants us to be holy; He doesn't wants us to go and acknowledged other god except Him (Leviticus 17:14)

Pleading the Blood of Jesus is a way to cleanse ourselves from all unknown evils, no one should wait to get to know what other people we have relationships with are doing before we free ourselves from errors they may be practising without us knowing it (See Leviticus 18 and see the prayers prayed by Psalmist David in Psalm 51)

> Have mercy upon me, O God, according to Your steadfast love; according to the multitude of Your tender mercy and loving-kindness blot out my transgressions. Wash me thoroughly [and repeatedly] from my iniquity and guilt and cleanse me and make me wholly pure from my sin! (Psalm 51:1-2)

I recommend to the reader of this book to read Psalm 51, in verse 1 to 2 of the same chapter, Psalmist David asked God to blot out his transgressions, each time we plead the blood of Jesus, what we are asking God to do for us is to blot out our transgressions, the only thing that can truly cleanse us from all sins is acknowledging the blood Jesus shed for us.

The Blood of Jesus is for Atonement: The Blood Our Saviour shed was and is to reconcile us to The Father God (see Leviticus 17:11 & Romans 3:24-26)

The Blood of Jesus is for Total Remission: it is for forgiveness from sins, for cleansing from all kind of evils, whether known or unknown (Hebrews 10)

The Blood of Jesus is for Protection: The Blood of Jesus is to protect us from all kind of evils, each time we plead the blood of Jesus, we are saying we come under the blood of Jesus for protection (Psalm 91)

The Blood of Jesus is What Give Us Freedom (Hebrews 10:20-22)

The Blood of Jesus healed us (Isaiah 53: 3-5)

The Blood of Jesus is what give us total victory over the works of satan (Revelation 12:11)

MOSES DISOBEYED GOD AND HE FACED THE CONSEQUENCE

And the Lord said to Moses, Take the rod, and assemble the congregation, you and Aaron your brother, and **tell the rock before their eyes to give forth its water,** and you shall bring forth to them water out of the rock; so you shall give the congregation and their livestock drink. So Moses took the rod from before the Lord, as He commanded him. And Moses and Aaron assembled the congregation before the rock and Moses said to them, Hear now, you rebels; must we bring you water out of this rock? And Moses lifted up his hand and with his rod he smote the rock twice. And the water came out abundantly, and the congregation drank, and their livestock.

And the Lord said to Moses and Aaron, Because you did not believe in (rely on, cling to) Me to sanctify Me in the eyes of the Israelites, you therefore shall not bring this congregation into the land which I have given them (Numbers 20:7-12)

Everyone must understand the season they are, the Bible advices that there is a time for everything in life (see Ecclesiastes 3). It is good to understand the season you are and what the Spirit of The Living God wants you to do.

God delights in us when we obey Him to the end. Moses did not get to the Promised Land because at a point during the journey, he did not follow God's commandments. God promised to bless them and to take them into their own land, but it require a good union with God through His Words.

Just as God commanded Moses, God still wants His Children to learn to say what He says. He wants each and every one of us to communicate with Him through praying His Words and His will into existence.

Chapter 4

WILDERNESS EXPERIENCE

When Pharaoh let the people go, God led them not by way of the land of the Philistines, although that was nearer; for God said, Lest the people change their purpose when they see war and return to Egypt. But God led the people around by way of the wilderness toward the Red Sea. And the Israelites went up marshalled [in ranks] out of the land of Egypt. (Exodus 13: 17-18)

Purpose Is Very Important.

God will do everything possible to truly lead His Children from every unpleasant situations. God was determined to save the children of Israel from slavery and He saved them from anything and everything that has the tendency of making them go back to what God was against. There is no error in Christ, God knew that if He chose a quicker route for the Children of Israel, there was a tendency for them to return into where God was taken them from. God know all things and He can see everything, therefore God's decision will always works in our favour not against us. We may not understand God's plans initially, but we must trust that though His plans seems longer, The Bible encourages us to wait for it; though it tarry, it will surely come.

> For the vision is yet for an appointed time and it hastens to the end [fulfillment]; it will not deceive or disappoint. Though it tarry, wait [earnestly] for it, because it will surely come; it will not be behindhand on its appointed day (Habakkuk 2:3)

God will not keep anyone in a solitary situations for ever, it is one of God's attributes to set people in captivity free, but there are moments when God would want to separate us from unnecessary distractions so as to align us with His blessings for us. If we are not used to solitary type of lifestyle, it may seems strange to us initially, but if we study carefully anyone who has made a good impact in our society, they've had moments of sacrificing time to hear the heartbeat of God concerning His purpose for their lives.   Some have paid the price of dedicating themselves to studying the Word of God and others have paid the price of dedicating and study resources that relates to their vocations. All of us must be willing to sacrifice some of our time to listen to what God has got to tell us and to be committed to a particular task God has set before us and to become an expert in our chosen fields.

Once we know the purpose to which God has called us, we must make it our ambitions to stay in it, putting some spirit of commitment and perseverance in our God's given assignment is very important and of good advantage to us as Christian. If we wants to avoid all forms of debt, poverty, lack and the tendency to be bankrupt, we should make it our habit to stay in our God's given purpose and assignment without wavering, we must dedicate ourselves to the right cause.

> ....but their nobles or lords did not put their necks to the work of their Lord (Nehemiah 3: 5b)

Coming out of bondage may require wilderness experience, wilderness experience is the time of solitude, time alone with God. It is the time when God reveals what He wants individuals to do to be truly and totally come out of all forms of bondages.

The wilderness experience may be the period that God wants you to start learning or studying something that will launch you into the everlasting blessings He has for you.

The wilderness experience may be when God will instil some discipline and His Laws in us, when He will mould our characters to conform to His will for us. It may be the moments God will develop in us the freedom from all forms of fears, agitating passions and moral conflicts, it may be the moments God will save us from some unknown troubles.

> Who were chosen and foreknown by God the Father and consecrated (sanctified, made holy) by the Spirit to be obedient to Jesus Christ (the Messiah) and to be sprinkled with [His] blood: May grace (spiritual blessing) and peace be given you in increasing abundance [that spiritual peace to be realized in and through Christ, freedom from fears, agitating passions, and moral conflicts] (1 Peter 1:2)

God may not rush to give you a quick, crumb eating, microwave blessings your flesh is craving for. He may take you through a journey that will lead into your Good Freedom, freedom from all forms of slavery, freedom from fears and freedom from all forms of evils.

Maybe, what satan has dished out for you all your life was crumbs level of blessings, maybe satan love to give you what he thinks you should have or what you deserved, or maybe he has tried to train your mind to settle for no blessings and he has given you thousands of reason why you should not bother to have your God ordained blessings.

God is saying to the reader of this book, you can truly be saved and be blessed, it may require an investment of time by you; time to study; time to become an expert in a God ordained purposes, it may require being dedicated or committed to a good cause.

God took the children of Israel through the wilderness experience so that they can be more matured and truly arrived at God's Good Purpose for their lives.

My prayer is that we shall all be sensitive to the Spirit of The Living God, if God is trying to slow us down or if He is trying to separate us from anything that may distract our attention from God, I pray that we will be more cooperate with The spirit of The Living God and instead of complaining, we will choose to listen to what the Spirit of The Living God is telling us.

Why The Waiting, Why The Longer Route, Why The Wilderness Experience?

The waiting moment is our training moment. It is a moment when God brings us into maturity necessary to handle the blessings He is bringing our ways, it is the time we develop an intimacy with God. It is a moment God develops character in us, it is a moment God will empower us to be dedicated to His good purpose for us.

> For I know the thoughts and plans that I have for you, says the Lord, thoughts and plans for welfare and peace and not for evil, to give you hope in your final outcome. (Jeremiah 29:11)

Coming Out of Bondage Will Require Walking in the Purpose of God

It delights God when we are at the centre of His will for us, God may not take us through the quick, microwave solutions that may not last. God's plan for us is to be in health and prosperity as our souls prospers.

> Beloved, I pray that you may prosper in every way and [that your body] may keep well, even as [I know] your soul keeps well and prospers. (3 John 1:2)

God's plan for us is to leave an inheritance for our children children (Prov.13:22)

Having a good purpose, being at the centre of God's will is very important to God. God did not take the children of Israel through a short, quick route because His plan was to establish them in a Good Enduring Wealth, and such wealth require a good training and the ability to endure. It requires having a Godly character, it requires having a good leadership skills. The blessings of The Lord is not a short term goals, it goes far more than one generation. Example was that of Abraham, Isaac and Jacob, and the blessings in their lives extends to Joseph and God's plan was to extend the blessings to the Israelites and He is extending the Covenant of Blessings to all The Christians today.

Prayer

If you are not sure of the reason why you are around, or you do not know God's plan for you, I will advise you to pray and seek God's face in prayer.

He will reveal to you that good plan He has for you. As soon as God reveals them:

*Write them down

*Write a Plan (A guide that will help you to evaluate your progress)

* Take a step of faith, little at a time, you may want to try your plan on a part time basis, if you like the result; you may want to continue to see your plan established or you may want to try something new, for an idea to start producing the good result we desired, it may take a good investment of time. If you have a full time job, do not resign from your job, try your new idea on a part time basis first.

*Whilst, we are trying to get our enterprise established, we must not be in a hurry to reap the profit while the business or the enterprise is trying to grow, we must remembered that our new venture may not be able to start paying us salary or profit in the early years of the venture but if we endure, then the blessings that follows a good dedications shall come to us in The Name of Jesus Christ (see Leviticus 19: 23-25)

And when you come into the land and have planted all kinds of trees for food, then you shall count the fruit of them as inedible and forbidden to you for three years; it shall not be eaten. In the fourth year all their fruit shall be holy for giving praise to the Lord. But in the fifth year you may eat of the fruit [of the trees], that their produce may enrich you; I am the Lord your God (Leviticus 19:23-25)

Prayer

Lord, save us from every small thinking mentality.

Lord, we receive Your Good Big plan for our lives, we withdraw ourselves from every small, insignificant ideas in The Name of Jesus Christ.

We receive the ability to think God's way and to think BIG in the Name of Jesus Christ.

We received the ability to have a long term significant goals in The Name of Jesus.

And He answered, It is not right (proper, becoming, or fair) to take the children's bread and throw it to the little dogs (Matthew 15:26)

If you have looked at yourself as puppies or you have fed on crumbs all your life, God is saying to you to come out of the lifestyle that doesn't matter or relevant by daily renewed your mind to conform to the Will and The Blessings of The Lord for you. The Bible advices that we must not conform to the patterns of this world, but to constant renewed our mind to align with the will of God. God is saying you should come out of slavery and start having a good plan for your life and allow your plans to be the one that can bless you and the people around you, we should all start thinking about Generational Blessings.

Instances in The Bible When People Experience Solitary Situations: God is Never Too Late

a. Noah waited in the ark for the flood to diminished (abate), after waiting; he sent a raven and a dove out on few occasions to check if it is save to come out of the Ark. **(The Bible recorded that Noah waited in the Ark for one year and ten days)** (Genesis 8) I hope the story of Noah will encourage someone and assure them to know that no matter how long you've been waiting for that breakthrough, God shall surely come through for you.

b. Joseph had a dream, it took him some wilderness experience before the dream became a reality (see the story of Joseph in Genesis 37 to 50)

c. The Children of Israel was in Egypt for several years before God sent them a deliverer to bring them out of Egypt into the Promised Land.

d. Though David was anointed as king of Israel, he waited for some years before he could take his position as king.

e. Jesus was in the wilderness for forty days and forty nights (Matthew 4)
f. Elizabeth secluded herself from the public for five months of the initial stages of her pregnancy (Luke 1:24)
g. John the Baptist was in the wilderness for some time until his commencement of the public ministry (Luke 1:80)
h. The disciples was advised to wait at Jerusalem until they were endued with power from high (Acts 1:4)
i. God made Saul (Apostle Paul) to wait until He sent Ananias to him to restore his sight (Acts 9)

We must all try to understand every stages we are at the journey of life. We must all turn every waiting moments to our preparation periods. We must remember that God has not forgotten us, He will surely come through and true for each and every one of us.

Chapter 5

GOD'S PRESENCE

The Lord went before them by day in a pillar of cloud to lead them along the way and by night in a pillar of fire to give them light, that they might travel by day and by night. The pillar of cloud by day and the pillar of fire by night did not depart from before the people (Exodus 13:20-22)

We must all remember that in the midst of all the challenging situations we may face, God is with us; and His presence shall not depart from us, also Exodus 23 emphasises that God's presence did not depart from the Children of Israel. I hope this give someone some peace of mind in the midst of their challenges that God is there. God is with you wherever you may go. The Bible says that God knows each and every one of us personally.

My covenant will I not break or profane, nor alter the thing that is gone out of My lips (Psalm 89:34)

Are not two little sparrows sold for a penny? And yet not one of them will fall to the ground without your Father's leave (consent) and notice. But even the very hairs of your head are all numbered. Fear not, then; you are of more value than many sparrows (Matthew 10: 29-31)

But in truth I tell you, there were many widows in Israel in the days of Elijah, when the heavens were closed up for three years and six months, so that there came a great famine over all the land. And yet Elijah was not sent to a single one of them, but only to Zarephath in the country of Sidon, to a woman who was a widow. And there were many lepers in Israel in the time of Elisha the prophet, and yet not one of them was cleansed [by being healed]—but only Naaman the Syrian (Luke 4: 2527)

*You are not alone in that situation, God is with you.

*Trust and be expecting God's Divine Protections in the midst of your waiting.

*Trust and be expecting God's Divine Intervention in the midst of your waiting.

*Trust and be expecting God's Divine Provisions in the midst of your journey.

*Trust and be expecting God's Divine Directions in the midst of your journey. *Anything that will last long may require a good investment of time on it, food that will taste good may require a good effort and time to prepare and cook it.

The Children of Israel may have accepted their conditions in Egypt as normal, maybe they have accepted the almost below average style as normal, but God showed up in their situations as The Almighty; the God that never forgets His covenant. To God their condition was not the best, it may looked normal to the Israelites, but God delivered them.

I will like to draw our attention to the story of Mary Magdalene and Mary (the mother) of James and Salome in the book of Mark 16, after the crucifixion of our Lord and Saviour Jesus, they both purchased sweet smelling spices to go and anoint Jesus body; on their way going they wondered who will help them to roll back the stone to enabled them to carry out their task, while they were contemplating about who will help them, they did not know that the stone was rolled back already; whilst the two of them were pondering over what seems like an obstacle before them, the obstacle was no longer there, Jesus was and is not in the graveyard, He has risen, the problem they were contemplating on was no longer there, it was resolved before they arrived at the destination. If your challenge looked like mountains, if it look large and it seems as if you will need a specialist to solve the problem, God in the midst of your challenge shall move all obstacles from your way in The Name of Jesus Christ. Whatever the task, whatever the challenge you faced, it will turn into a good testimony for you. It will result in you rejoicing in The Name of Jesus Christ.

> And they said to one another, Who will roll back the stone for us out of [the groove across the floor at] the door of the tomb? And when they looked up, they [distinctly] saw that the stone was already rolled back, for it was very large. (Mark 16:3-4)

> And he said to them, Do not be amazed and terrified; you are looking for Jesus of Nazareth, Who was crucified. He has risen; He is not here. See the place where they laid Him. But be going; tell the disciples and Peter, He goes before you into Galilee; you will see Him there, [just] as He told you. (Mark 16:6-7)

Prayer

I say to the reader of this book, The Lord God will send His angels your way to make room for you and simplify your work in The Name of Jesus Christ. Before you arrived at your point of challenge, God will be there before you, making ways for you, making you to ride on your high places with no struggles in the Name of Jesus Christ.

The Lord God will go before you and make all forms of crookedness straight in the Name of Jesus Christ:

Every valley shall be lifted and filled up, and every mountain and hill shall be made low; and the crooked and uneven shall be made straight and level, and the rough places a plain. And the glory (majesty and splendour) of the Lord shall be revealed, and all flesh shall see it together; for the mouth of the Lord has spoken it. (Isaiah 40:4-5)

Joshua was worried when he took over the task of taking the Israelites to the Promised Land, because they were all used to Moses pleading their cases before the Lord, but God spoke to Joshua in the midst of his worries. Joshua was worried because the task of leadership was carried by Moses throughout their journey; Moses interceded for them several times, but God assured Joshua that He was the one who empowered Moses, and He can do the same for anyone. Therefore for the task before you, be encouraged and trust in the Lord God; He will not disappoint you.

…….. As I was with Moses, so I will be with you; I will not fail you or forsake you (Joshua 1:5b)

Prayer

Those looking for you in the graveyard, those looking for you in the house of bondage; those looking for you in the house of poverty and lack shall not find you there anymore in The Name of Jesus Christ. Only the sound of rejoicing shall be found in your assemblies in The Name of Jesus Christ.

God is Never Too Late

> The Lord went before them by day in a pillar of cloud to lead them along the way and by night in a pillar of fire to give them light, that they might travel by day and by night. The pillar of cloud by day and the pillar of fire by night did not depart from before the people (Exodus 13:21-22)

God is never too late, whatever the season of life you may be, whether in the early, middle or later season of life the Lord God shall come through for you in The Name of Jesus Christ.

If you are going through some challenges, God will come through for you. He is capable of providing everything you will need to make it through in life.

BE HOPEFUL: God is capable of making anyone to be fruitful even in the night season of life. No one is too young or too old to be used and be blessed by the Lord, therefore on that your good plan, do not give up on it, GOD'S BLESSINGS IS NEVER TOO LATE.

Some Instances in The Bible Where God Came Through For His People

Throughout the Bible and till today and forever God answered the prayers of His people.

a. Noah waited in The Ark for the floods to abate, while waiting, He sent a raven out to check if it was okay for them to come out of the Ark. God eventually remembered Noah (Genesis 8)

b. The Lord God answered the prayer of Sarah (Genesis 21:2)

c. The Lord God answered the prayer of Isaac and gave Rebekah children
(Genesis 25:21)

d. And The Lord remembered Rachel and gave her children (Genesis 30: 22)

e. The Lord God answered the prayers of the Israelites whist in Egypt and He sent
Moses to lead them out of Egypt (Exodus 3:7-8)

f. The Lord God came through for Joseph eventually

g. The Lord God came through for Ruth and Naomi

h. The Lord God remembered Daniel in the Lion's den.

i. The Lord God answered the prayer of Zachariah and Elizabeth after they have been tagged as barren (Luke 1)

j. The Lord God remembered and answered the prayers of Prophetess Anna after been a widow for eighty four years and she returned thanks to God and talked of Jesus to everyone looking for redemption (Luke 2:36-38)

k. Helps was eventually sent to Saul who later became Paul to restore his sight (Acts 9)

l. God sent His angels to go and release Peter from prison (Acts 12)

m. Paul and Silas was freed from prison (Acts 16)

You Have No Excuse to Fail

God will come through for each and every one of us, do not give up, use your waiting moment to develop yourself, study and receive illuminations from God. Remember your case is not hopeless, as soon as God is ready to bring you out of the unpleasant situations into a better living standard, nothing can stop Him. Your educational background cannot stop God and you cannot stop God from blessing you. God is a God that looks beyond someone's fault to qualify for His blessings, therefore be willing and obedient and God will perfect that which concerns you.

> Now when they saw the boldness and unfettered eloquence of Peter and John and perceived that they were unlearned and untrained in the schools [common men with no educational advantages], they marveled; and they recognized that they had been with Jesus (Acts 4:13)

> And Moses said to the Lord, O Lord, I am not eloquent or a man of words, neither before nor since You have spoken to Your servant; for I am slow of speech and have a heavy and awkward tongue. And the Lord said to him, Who has made man's mouth? Or who makes the dumb, or the deaf, or the seeing, or the blind? Is it not I, the Lord? Now therefore go, and I will be with your mouth and will teach you what you shall say (Exodus 4: 10-12)

The story of Moses painted the picture of how human beings behaved generally, we all tends to have one reason or the other why we believe that some blessings is for certain group of people, or that some blessings is too much for us, be encouraged to give yourself to studying and training to become the best God designed you to be. God called Moses to be a deliverer in helping to bring the Israelites out of Egypt, Moses complained because he was looking at His inadequacy, he did not think initially about

Gods adequacy, but we thank God, He looked beyond Moses excuses and God still used him and it was recorded that the same Moses was educated in all the wisdom required for him to carry out his assignment. God can perfect that which concerns anyone.

Therefore, I encourage the reader of this book to start, even if your knowledge in your
God's given assignment is at almost zero level, God is capable of teaching and training you to become the expert He destined you to be for Him.

> So Moses was educated in all the wisdom and culture of the Egyptians, and he was mighty (powerful) in his speech and deeds (Acts 7:22)

Another example of how God can used anyone to bless them and to bring glory to Himself is in the story of Peter and John, the Bible recorded that they were unlearned and untrained in the schools, they were everyday people just like you and me and God poured His Wisdom on them and mighty miracles was performed through their hands. God is looking for someone who is willing and obedient and the Bible says such shall eat the best of the land.

> Now when they saw the boldness and unfettered eloquence of Peter and John and perceived that they were unlearned and untrained in the schools [common men with no educational advantages], they marvelled; and they recognized that they had been with Jesus (Acts 4:13)

Chapter 6

THE RED SEA EXPERIENCE

Fear not; stand still (firm, confident, undismayed) and see the salvation of the Lord which He will work for you today. For the Egyptians you have seen today you shall never see again (Exodus 14:13)

How many of us has wondered why should God allowed the children of Israel to go through the red sea, didn't God knew the red sea was there? God Knew the red sea was there, He made them to pass through the Red Sea so as to show that God can conquered any obstacles, to encourage someone to always attempt something great for God.

God is aware of the oppositions, obstacles or any financial challenges you may face on your journey to The Promised Blessings. The moments of obstacles are the moments when God will show His Almightiness. Do not be scared of any red sea or giants you may encounter on your way,

God is in the midst of your battles and He will see you through. Be encouraged to think big and to be willing to face your Red Seas, do not run away; do not shrink back in fear.

God does not want us to settle for a little, insignificant, no challenge easy to achieve dreams kind of lifestyle, we must all be willing to attempt something great for God.

To be encouraged, I will advise us to study the story of David vs Goliath in the book of 1 Samuel Chapter 17. David did not ran away from Goliath, the Bible wrote that David ran towards Goliath in the battle despite the fact that king Saul referred to David as only adolescent (1 Samuel 17:33) David ceased the opportunity presented before him, he fought the battle with Goliath and David conquered (1Samuel 17: 48-50)

My prayer is that no one among us will run away from the challenges that will lead to us being blessed in The Name of Jesus Christ.

Say: I shall no longer be scared of any red seas situations in The Name of Jesus Christ.

The Lord God will empowered us to face the red sea whenever possible knowing that the victory is sure in The Name of Jesus Christ.

Caution:

Before you attempt to face a mighty sea or challenge for God, be sure that:

**You are at the centre of His will for you

**Make sure that your covenant with God is intact

**Pay your tithes regularly to a God ordained ministry that teaches the Word of God

**Serve in your local church and other God's approved ministries.

**Study the Word of God regularly.

Do not go to battle alone, make sure you are in good accord with God. This will give you more confident that God's presence will always be there with you from the beginning to the end and even after the battle is won. I am sure the Children of Israel would have preferred the route where there was no red sea, but God had to train them on how to accept challenges in life and how to fight and win. God wants us to THINK BIG, to think and dream like Him.

START THINKING BIG

Pray that God will give you a dream that you cannot accomplish without Him.

Pray that God will give you a Dream and Projects that will terminate sorrows and shame from your life.

Pray that God will give you dreams and visions that can pay your bills in The Name of Jesus Christ.

Pray that God's purpose and Blessings coming your way will be big enough to result in you being blessed and God being praised in The Name of Jesus Christ. (1 Samuel 17:26)

Pray and ask God for a GIANT SIZE DREAMS that terminate ridicules in Jesus Mighty Name.

Pray that your vision, your spouse's vision; your children's visions and your family and friend's visions shall matters, significant and speaks God's Blessings in The Name of Jesus Christ.

Pray that God will lead you into a GIANT SIZE CHALLENGES in the Name of Jesus Christ.

SAY THESE OUT LOUD:

Lord, give me my mountains (see the story of Caleb in Joshua 14)

I refuse to die small

I shall not die small

I do not want crumbs

I Am a Giant Killer

In My Light shall Nations see Light in The Name of Jesus Christ

I have the mind-set of God The Almighty

I am not a bastard, I think Big like my Daddy (God)

I break through walls

I break through the walls of oppositions

I break through the walls of satanic embargoes

I break through the walls of impossible situations in The Name of Jesus Christ.

I resign from the spirits of small thinking, crumbs eating mentality.

I moved to the realm of surplus blessings in The Name of Jesus Christ

I walked into my Promised Blessings in The Name of Jesus Christ

I shall not see Pharaoh and the Red sea again

Every mountains of obstacles to my blessings have crumbled in The Name of Jesus Christ

The Red seas of poverty is over in The Name of Jesus Christ

The Red seas of sickness is over in The Name of Jesus Christ

The Red seas of death is over in The Name of Jesus Christ

I entered into my lifetime of abundant blessings and uncommon favours in the Name of Jesus Christ

I shall not lack anything good in The Name of Jesus Christ

I received my abundant blessings and favours in The Name of Jesus Christ.

Chapter 7

BEING ON FIRE FOR GOD

The Lord went before them by day in a pillar of cloud to lead them along the way and by night in a pillar of fire to give them light, that they might travel by day and by night. The pillar of cloud by day and the pillar of fire by night did not depart from before the people. (Exodus 13: 21-22)

Fire is for purification, it is for sanctification, it gives directions, and fire is used sometimes to separate the pure from the impure. We were advised to keep pressing into the best God has for us, we are to allow the Word of God to purify us until we come forth as gold. To check the genuines of gold, it has to be able to go through some levels of fire, we are to allow The Word of God to dwell in us richly so that when we go through the storms of life, **we shall still be standing after the storms are over**. Daniel's friends (Shadrach, Meshach and Abednego) faith was tested by fire and they came out of the fire successfully (see Daniel 3:27)

> I will send my messenger, who will prepare the way before me. Then suddenly the Lord you are seeking will come to his temple; the messenger of the covenant, whom you desire, will come, says the Lord Almighty. But who can endure the day of his coming? Who can stand when he appears? For he will be like a refiner's fire or a launderer's soap. He will sit as a refiner and purifier of silver; he will purify the Levites and refine them like gold and silver. Then the Lord will have men who will bring offerings in righteousness, and the offerings of Judah and Jerusalem will be acceptable to the Lord, as in days gone by, as in former years (Malachi 3:1-4)

God does not walk around with no fire in Him, in fact the Bible told us that He dwells in the midst of fire (see Exodus 3:1-5). Whatever your situations, whatever your challenges; be expecting some Holy Ghost Fire that will move you into the realm of miraculous in The Name of Jesus Christ.

Be expecting some Holy Ghost Fire that will change every wrong pursuit in your life to a Good God Ordained Purposes in the Name of Jesus Christ.

The scripture from the Malachi 3 above emphasises that God will purify and cleanse us, for God is like a Refiner's

Fire or A Launderer's Soap and that He will refined us until we become like gold and silver.

> I know your [record of] works and what you are doing; you are neither cold nor hot. Would that you were cold or hot! So, because you are lukewarm and neither cold nor hot, will I spew you out of My mouth! (Revelation 3:15-16)

I pray that God in His Infinite Mercy will grant us the grace to stay constantly at the middle of His will for us. His fire around us will burn and terminate from us every wrong spirits in The Name of Jesus Christ.

I pray that no one will be disqualified from their God ordained purposes in The Name of Jesus Christ. The Lord God will renewed our strength daily better than that of the eagles. Even, where we think we are not capable, even where errors is trying to attract and distract us, God Almighty will prove Himself bigger than any errors in The Name of Jesus Christ.

God will not associate with anyone or anything that is not hot and on fire for Him. We must love His Laws and all His precepts. We must be willing to work hard and to work smart managing Gods resources well, we must not be lazy. If God is rejecting lukewarmness, if God is rejecting an average lifestyle, then we ought to be like our Father God. We ought to be on fire for God by pressing on to achieve the best God has purposed for us to enjoy in the land of the living.

Exodus 13:21 explained to us that God went with the Children of Israel in a pillar of cloud to lead them along their journey by day and the pillar of fire to give them light by night that they might travel by day and by night. This particular verse shows that God doesn't approve passivity. He wants us to be fruitful at all times, we should not have any excuses to fail in life. If God can make provisions for us to make things not too difficult for us, then we should cooperate with God by being willing to be more productive. Listening to the Word of God regularly is a good way to have access to the fire and the cloud that God will provide for us which was what we discussed in the earlier chapters of this book, i.e. to have regular fellowship with God. In God's presence is the fullness of joy (Psalm 16:11). In the presence of God is where all the satanic chains will be broken from us in The Name of Jesus Christ. No one will go back into the dirt of the past in The Name of Jesus Christ. The Lord God said to the Israelites "The Battles they have seen , they shall not see again and it was not recorded that they see the red sea again, so shall it be for each and every one of us, we shall not go back to the spirit of unbelieving again in The Name of Jesus.

Being on fire for God require constant listening to His Word and studying it, believing and receiving them for ourselves, not using it against anyone, knowing that we do not wrestle against flesh and blood but against

every wicked spirit that may not want us to attain the best God has for us. God love all souls including the gentiles, He died so that they too can become the Children of God, so that everyone can be qualified as the Children of God. He wrote in the Bible "I came to seek that which was lost" (Luke 19:10)

The Light of The Word of God must be switched on constantly in our homes, in our lives, in our cities, this is what God wants, and this is The God's Plan for His People.

The Anointing Oil

> You shall command the Israelites to provide you with pure oil of crushed olives for the light, to cause it to burn continually [every night]. In the Tent of Meeting [of God with His people], outside the veil which sets apart the Testimony, Aaron and his sons shall keep it burning from evening to morning before the Lord. It shall be a statute to be observed on behalf of the Israelites throughout their generations. (Exodus 27:20-21)

The Anointing Oil represents progress, progress in all our God's Ordained Purpose, progress to be on fire for Christ. I pray that our lives shall not lack the Oil from God's presence in The Name of Jesus Christ.

The Rewards of Being on Fire for God

Good rewards attends to those whose mind stayed on God, He promised to keep them in perfect state where they can function appropriately for Him (see Isaiah 26:3)

The Bible teaches us that as Christ is so we are and it emphasises that we are joint heirs with Christ, we are seated together with God.

> In this [union and communion with Him] love is brought to completion and attains perfection with us, that we may have confidence for the day of judgment [with assurance and boldness to face Him], because as He is, so are we in this world (1 John 4:17)

> And He raised us up together with Him and made us sit down together [giving us joint seating with Him] in the heavenly sphere [by virtue of our being] in Christ Jesus (the Messiah, the Anointed One) (Ephesians 2:6)

Therefore we must all be willing to take our positions of:

Blessings

Honour

Majesty

Glory

Splendour

All the Power

Riches

Wisdom

Might

Dominion

And You have made them a kingdom (royal race) and priests to our God, and they shall reign [as kings] over the earth! Then I looked, and I heard the voices of many angels on every side of the throne and of the living creatures and the elders [of the heavenly Sanhedrin], and they numbered ten thousand times ten thousand and thousands of thousands, Saying in a loud voice, Deserving is the Lamb, Who was sacrificed, to receive all the power and riches and wisdom and might and honour and majesty (glory, splendour) and blessing! And I heard every created thing in heaven and on earth and under the earth [in Hades, the place of departed spirits] and on the sea and all that is in it, crying out together, To Him Who is seated on the throne and to the Lamb be ascribed the blessing and the honour and the majesty (glory, splendour) and the power (might and dominion) forever and ever

(through the eternities of the eternities)! (Revelation 5:10-13)

LORD LET YOUR FIRE FALLS

The fire of God's presence is the Word of God, The Fire of God is the Light of God. It is to bring Total Salvation to Souls Everywhere. Only God knows the numbers of souls that would be saved by one Divine Interventions. The day Moses saw God's fire was when his destiny begins. The fire of God's presence was what change Saul to Paul, from murderer to deliverer.

(See Exodus 3:1-5, Acts 9:1-18, 1 Kings 18)

Prayer

Lord let Your fire falls to stop evils in our land. Lord let Your fire falls to stop iniquities in our land.

Lord let Your fire falls to connect souls back to The Word of God.

Lord, let Your fire falls to restore souls back to Your Blessings for their lives.

Lord let Your fire falls to stop the attacks on the

Christians everywhere. Lord let Your fire falls to

blind satan and its agents.

Lord let Your fire falls (say this 20 times)

Lord let Your fire falls to stop the works of satan in The Name of Jesus Christ.

Lord let Your fire falls to give Divine Directions.

Lord let Your fire falls to give sight to the blind: Acts 9:17

Lord removes scales from people's eyes that has been stopping them from accepting Christ as their Lord and Saviour (Acts 9:18)

Lord, let there be a visible evidence that will convince people that their salvation is in Christ Jesus (Acts 9:21)

Lord, connects Christians; gives us the abilities to be able to work together (Acts 9: 19b)

Lord release into the lives of all Christians the strong convictions that will makes us to pursue our Assignments relentlessly in The Name of Jesus Christ.

Lord, let the fire of Your presence fall. The fire that will make us to start pursuing our God's Given Assignments in The Name of Jesus Christ.

Lord, let Your fire falls. The fire of Your presence that will take us from being an ordinary to an extraordinary for God.

The fire that will disconnect us from wrong associations and connect us to the right associations.

Lord let the fire of Your presence falls on me to remove satanic scales from my eyes.

Lord let Your fire fall to stop the works of satan in my life.

Lord, let Your fire falls to stop the works of satan in our lands.

THE FIRE OF GODS BLESSINGS

THE FIRE OF GODS HEALING POWER

THE FIRE OF CELEBRATIONS

Lord; let Your fire fall on me

Lord let Your fire fall on everything that belongs to me

Lord let Your fire falls in our community

Lord let Your fire falls in our Nations

Lord let Your fire falls in our churches

Lord let Your fire falls on our congregations

Lord let Your fire falls to stop us from pursuing the wrong goals. Lord let Your fire falls to stop us from going the wrong directions.

Lord let Your fire falls to bring Divine transformations to our lives.

Lord let Your fire falls into the lives of my children to lead them to Your Blessings and Wisdom.

Notes:

The day Moses saw Your fire was when his destiny begins

The fire of Your presence was what changed Saul to Paul, from murderer to deliverer.

Lord let Your fire falls to accelerate me to accomplish great assignments in Your Name.

Lord let Your fire fall to separate me and start preparing me for greatness.

THE FIRE OF GODS PRESENCE IS THE FIRE OF THE WORD OF GOD

Lord, let Your fire fall to separate me into a life of significant, a life that matter, a life that is relevant.

Father let Your fire fall on me for the whole world to see Your Glory in my life.

Father let Your fire fall on me to beautify me, to sanctify me.

Father let Your fire fall on me to make me to start possessing my possessions.

Father Let Your fire fall to bring beautifications into my life

To bring beautification into our society

To bring glorifications

To bring Divine Assignments

To bring Divine improvements into my life

The fire of strength

The Fire of Deliverance from bondages

The Fire of Freedom from satanic oppressions and depressions

The Fire to stop errors

The Fire to stop sadness

The Fire to stop poverty and lack

The Fire of Divine interventions

The Fire of Divine Breakthroughs

The fire of The Mercy of God

The Fire of Wisdom of God

The fire of The Peace of Mind

The fire of the joy of The Lord

The Fire of Divine Connections to Blessings

The fire of Divine Directions to Blessings

The fire of Divine Assignments

Lord let Your fire falls in my home

Lord let Your fire falls in my Ministry

Lord let Your fire falls to revive us

Lord let Your fire falls to stop wastage; to stop acts of dirtiness

Lord let Your fire falls to stop idleness; to stop laziness

Lord let Your fire falls to stop ignorance

Lord let your fire falls to stop poverty

Lord let Your fire falls to stop lack; to stop isolations

To stop grieves

To silent sickness

To stop death

The Fire of God to bring Divine Love

To Bring Brotherly Kindness

To Bring Salvation

To Bring Purity

To Bring Holiness

To Bring Strength

To Bring Directions

To Bring Fruitfulness

To Bring Wisdom

To Bring Justice

To Bring Godly Kindness

To Bring Divine Provisions

To Bring Orders and Discipline

To Bring Security

To bring Godly Visions

To bring Godly Ideas

To bring Deliverance from Captivity

To Bring Deliverance from Ignorance

To bring deliverance from Bondages

To bring Deliverance from slaveries

To bring resurrections of families

To bring resurrection of

Godly   relationships

NOTE:

Moses witness the fire of God and never remain the same (Exodus 3)

Samson witness the fire and receive deliverance and was set free (Judges 15: 13-14)

Saul experience The Fire of God, his wrong

motives was changed (Acts 9) I receive the fire of

God into my life.

NOTE:

The Word of God is the fire (Jeremiah 5:14)

> Therefore thus says the Lord God of hosts: Because you [the people] have spoken this word, behold, I will make My words fire in your mouth ....(Jeremiah 5:14)

THE FIRE THAT IS NOT FROM GOD IS DESTROYED IN THE NAME OF JESUS
CHRIST (see Leviticus 10:1-3)

Any system, every ideas that is not of God shall not be kindle for my sake in The Name of Jesus Christ.

Every wrong fires are destroyed, their powers broken and stopped in the Name of Jesus Christ.

The Fire of His presence doesn't kill God's Own Elects (But it can kill God's enemies) see: (Daniel 3: 22-30) though the fire in the Book of Daniel was set up by an earthly king; **it has no power over the Children of God**. We must all desire to be on Gods side at all times by choosing to give ourselves to study The Word of God, to find out what God is saying, to serve God and to do His will. I pray that satan shall not speak to me, satan shall not speak to my children, satan shall not speak to my family and friends. I refuse to bow to idols. I received deliverance from every wrong doctrines, I received deliverance from every wrong associations. I receive deliverance from every wrong influences, and satan shall not have authority over me in The Name of Jesus Christ.

Examples of When The Wrong Fires Fails in The Lives of The Children of God.

**What King Nebuchadnezzar did in the Book of Daniel 3 was that, he sets up Golden

Images for people to worship and bow down to it and all who refused to bowed, he promised to set them on fire; but the fire sets up by satan has no power over the Children of God. This is my report, that satans power is useless, its controlling powers are destroyed in The Name of Jesus Christ.

Whatever has bowed our heads down unnecessarily for generations, received the judgements of God in the Name of Jesus Christ. Systems have been changed to favour us, favours have been released into my life. I receive Fresh Oil to continue to proclaim my Salvations in Christ without looking back, without feeling guilty in The Name of Jesus Christ. I refuse satanic distractions in The name of Jesus Christ. I received strength, joy, life; health, beauty and the ability of being renewed to manifest the glory and honour of The Lord.

I shall not bow to adversities, I shall not bow to death; I shall not bow to sin; I shall not bow to lack; I shall not bow to poverty; I shall not bow to sickness in The Name of Jesus Christ.

Satanic doors have been shut right now for my sake, for the sake of my children; families and friends; regrets become the portion of whatever has bowed our heads down from today in The Name of Jesus Christ. I walk tall, with confidence in The Lord. I received wealth being transferred unto me, I received honours being transferred unto me. The works of satan shall not work, its light refuse to come up; the flames of satan is quenched in Nations in The Name of Jesus Christ. Satans agents are released into hell in The name of Jesus Christ, all the agents of satan becomes blind and dumb for my sake from today in The name of Jesus Christ. I receive new strength to be able to fight and fight the good fight of faith in The Name of Jesus Christ.

Spirit of fears; errors; satanic embargos; your powers are broken beyond repairs for my sake, in The Name of Jesus Christ.

Tears are been wiped away from people's faces worldwide in The Name of Jesus Christ. The Flames of satan goes off in our Nations in The Name of Jesus Christ (amen)

WHAT WE NEED IS NOT THE FIRE FROM HELL, BUT THE FIRE FROM GODS PRESENCE

Fire from the pit of hell is destroyed for my sake, Lord, opens my eyes to see what satan and its cohorts were trying to do and show me the escape route to Salvation. Fires that the earthly kings and humans have sets up will not have powers over me; it will not have powers over my children and my families in The Name of Jesus.

From today I walk into my prepared blessings in The Name of Jesus Christ.

The Genuine Fire of God's presence usually delivers His Own from troubles. The Fire of God's presence doesn't kills, and it gives sight to the blinds. It gives directions, it gives instructions, it gives divine protections from all evils (1 Kings 17: 1-24)

The Fire of God's presence revive souls, it gives lives to what satan is trying to kill in our lives (1 Kings 17:22)

Prayer

Lord God, I pray that the right fire will remain in Nations and every wrong fire to be switched off in The Name of Jesus Christ.

THE FIRE FROM GOD IS FOR DIVINE PROTECTIONS (2 Kings 1:1-10)

Thank You Lord God for filling us with Your presence and with Your power. Thank You for making the whole world, every system, every spirit know that they could not and cannot do me no harm. Thank You, Lord God for Your Faithfulness to me, to my spouse; to my children; to my congregations.

THANK YOU LORD GOD FOR YOUR FAITHFULNESS TO ME

Thank You Lord God for the Demonstrations of Your Power in our midst.

Thank You Lord God for being faithful to Your Word, thank You Lord God for Your Divine Coverings on Your Ministers.

NOTE: Seek your counsel from The Lord God only, do not seek counsel from any medium, do not seek counsel or helps from any idol. Lord, opens our eyes to see the men of God You are sending our ways. Anoint us to honour them in The Name of Jesus Christ.

Prayer

Lord anoint us to immerse ourselves in Your Word

Lord Anoint us not to seek

counsels in the wrong places, Lord

break down every rod and the

spirits of offence for us,

Lord anoints us so that no offence will have power over us.

SAME FIRE DIFFERENT RESULTS: (See Daniel 3)

I receive the empowerments to refuse to bow to wrong doctrines, I receive the empowerments to refuse to bow to wrong influence.

I receive the empowerments to stand for the cause of Christ in the face of challenges. I release the fire of God to roast and destroy evils that may want to come near my habitations in The name of Jesus Christ. I release the fire of God to roast to pieces anything that wants to subject me and my children to the lives of poverty.

Father God, I pray that Your Fire in Me will not be quench in The Name of Jesus Christ. No one will be able to switch off The Flame of God in me and in my children.

I shall not bow to evil in The Name of Jesus Christ.

CHARIOTS OF FIRE

Same Fire that gives sight is the same Fire that can silence the works of satan: 2 Kings 6:17-22 also see Acts 9.

Lord surrounds me with The Fire from Your Presence

Lord surrounds everything that belongs to me with The fire from Your Presence

Lord let the Fire from Your Presence silence the works of satan in my environments

Lord let the fire from Your Presence fills Nations

Lord let the fire from Your Presence silent satan in Nations in The Name of Jesus Christ

Lord let the fire from Your Presence removes evils and errors for my sake.

Lord sends blindness to every wrong vision in my environments.

Lord silent wrong visions and ideas for my spouse.

Lord silent wrong visions and ideas for my children.

Lord, give every wrong visions; time wasting dreams wrong directions away from me and my loved ones. Lord silent every wrong pursuit for us.

Lord, send confusions to the camp of satan on my behalf.

Lord, leads evil away from my habitations; evils will not find me; evils will not find my children in The Name of Jesus Christ.

Chapter 8

MAKING GOOD WHERE YOU ARE

And they said to Moses, The people bring much more than enough for doing the work which the Lord commanded to do. So Moses commanded and it was proclaimed in all the camp, let no man or woman do anything more for the sanctuary offering. So the people were restrained from bringing. For the stuff they had was sufficient to do all the work and more Exodus 36: 5-7

As I have explained at the beginning of this book, coming Out of bondage may not necessarily mean relocating to another geographical location and it may mean relocating to where God wants you to be. Whichever one applies to you, God want you to make good use of every resources and every opportunities available to you to achieve His purpose for you, so as to meet your needs and to advance His kingdom. If God is saying to you to enjoy where you are on your way to where He is taking you, then do so, but remembered to move as soon as He ask you to do so.

Do not wait till when you get to the Promised Land before you start doing something worthwhile to make you start enjoying the best God has for you. From the day one God sent Moses to announce His plan to take the children of God to the promised land, they never stopped doing something to advance their journey; whilst still on the journey the Israelites gave Moses a freewill offerings to build the sanctuary for the service unto the Lord (freewill offerings doesn't come from the idle hands) and the Bible recorded that they gave so much, Moses had to command that they should stop bringing offerings because they had too much for the work.

From this story we learn that we should not be laid back, idle, doing nothing and waiting for The Promised Land to come. Taking from the stories of The Israelites coming out of Egypt, the first thing God did was to give them an assignment, I pray that each and every one of us will be willing to accept our God's given responsibilities in The Name of Jesus Christ.

Each man was to go and solicit from his neighbours jewels of silver and jewels of gold (Exodus 11:2-3) meaning we have to be more resourceful, not to go on robbery, but to dress clean and not to dress as if we were already defeated or frustrated. If you have good mindset that God is taking you into the Promised Land, then you do not need to feel frustrated, you do not need to start wearing rags. You can start wearing clean clothes, having a regular good showers, nice hair cut or moderate and beautiful hairstyle. You can wear moderate jewellery and make up that is not too expensive. No situations should make anyone feel downcast to the extent that nobody would like to employ them, shake off all the spirit of rejections and abuse in The Name of Jesus Christ. May God leads someone to where they can find divine encouragements to start pursuing their God's given assignments in The Name of Jesus Christ. No sadness and any form of worthlessness will attend to you again in The Name of Jesus Christ and before you whisper your prayers, God will answer you in The Name of Jesus Christ. What satan has stolen from you all your lifetime shall be restored to you in one day in The Name of Jesus Christ.

We have to open our eyes and our minds to find out what is available for us wherever we find ourselves such as:

What training is available?

What job is available?

Who needs my helps?

Who needs my services?

What Trade or Business can I start?

What voluntary work can I give?

What is the help the government is providing to eradicate poverty in my city that I can tap into?

Like the Children of Israel, we must be willing to follow God's direction.

God is willing to bless you where you are, coming out of bondage does not necessarily means relocating to another city, it may means: being willing to see your life being blessed abundantly according to the will of God, it may means being diligent where you are in your God's given assignment. It may means being willing to prosper according to the will of God.

God brought the children of Israel out of the Egypt, on their way to The Promised Land, The Lord God empowered them, He enriched them and gave them more than enough blessings to meet their needs, **Moses has to restrained the Israelites from bringing sanctuary offerings for the work of the sanctuary,** to prepare it for service because the people brought sufficient stuff to do all the work. Someone may be wondering, shouldn't they be sleeping or waiting till when they will get into the Promised Land and the works will begin, shouldn't they continue to keep praying for God's miracle without doing anything. God doesn't work like that, your miracle, breakthrough and blessings starts where you are, it is tied to you being able to hear God and obey Him.

Stop Waiting, Start Doing

To truly break the backbone of poverty, we must be willing to accept our God's given assignments, the Bible advices us that whatever your hands finds to do in goodness, do it.

> Go your way, eat your bread with joy, and drink your wine with a cheerful heart [if you are righteous, wise, and in the hands of God], for God has already accepted your works. Let your garments be always white [with purity], and let your head not lack [the] oil [of gladness]. Live joyfully with the wife whom you love ………………... Whatever your hand finds to do, do it with all your might ……………... (Ecclesiastes 9:7-10)

If God can empowered those on a journey, if He can empowered the Israelites whilst in the wilderness, then God can bless anyone anywhere. This brought back my memory as a child growing up in a capital of a state in Nigeria. My biological Dad was a Builder of houses by profession, but at the same time he had three sites for farming, two for regular farming and one for cocoa. I and my siblings often follows him to the farm to go and collect foodstuffs, but on our way to my dad's farming sites, along the ways were various trees with fruits growing on them, mostly guava and oranges, most of the time no one harvested the fruits on the trees and the fruits usually drops on the ground by themselves, because the owners of the lands doesn't cultivate and harvest their lands or maybe the lands doesn't belongs to anyone. The picture God is trying to show us from this story is the spirit of abundance, the spirit of more than enough, the spirits of sufficiency. I believe this type of blessings was what the Israelites encountered on their ways to the Promised Land, the Israelites enjoyed the blessings and the provisions of God The Almighty on their way to the Promised Land, on a particular occasion God rained down manna for them from heaven. God is still alive today, the end will not come until we have all enjoyed and experience the overflowing blessings of the Lord that is possible for everyone in The Name of Jesus Christ. If God supplies the needs before, He will definitely meet the needs again. The kind of freewill blessings, the kind of sweatless victory, the kind of more than enough blessings, the good doors that opened of their own accords will be each and every one of us experiences in The Name of Jesus Christ, the days of labouring hard with no result is over in The Name of Jesus Christ.

YOUR MIRACLES BEGINS WHERE YOU ARE

With God nothing is ever impossible (Luke 1:37-38) Develop a good mindset that anywhere you find yourself, every opportunities you have to become somebody, you will cease it, you will enjoy the blessings of the Lord with no limits in The Name of Jesus Christ. You will have the mindset that life in abundant that God promised us is possible in the land of the living (John 10:10)

The day of your slavery has ended, you shall no longer beg for crumbs in The Name of Jesus Christ.

God Will Defends You If He Is Sending You

> And Jesus replied to them, saying, Have you never so much as read what David did when he was hungry, he and those who were with him? — How he went into the house of God and took and ate the [sacred] loaves of the showbread, which it is not permitted for any except only the priests to eat, and also gave to those [who were] with him? And He said to them, The Son of Man is Lord even of the Sabbath (Luke 6:3-5)

This passage of the Bible is not to encourage robbery in our midst but to conquer the spirit of fear that may want anyone to draw back away from pressing towards the blessings of The Lord for them, to give someone the peace of mind if satan is trying to threatens them that some God Ordained jobs or blessings is too much for them, especially if they have waited for several years to experience the blessings of The Lord.

Being constantly choosing to listen to the Word of God will save us from lots of known and unknown troubles, let people in your environment know that you belong to Jesus

Christ, do not hide your faith from anyone, Jesus Christ called us to be a good witness for Him.

He has not called us into a life of robbery, the above verse is to encourage us to silence all the condemning spirits that tries to stop The Christians to be the best that God has called them to be, and it is to encourage someone to take good steps towards being the best for God. It is in other to stop all forms of wrong doctrines for their sakes, it is to encourage and re-establish the FREEDOM we have in Christ. If a thousand voices is trying to tell you that some blessings is too good for you, just remember Luke 6:3-5 and says though by the natural laws and to men it may look impossible to have the best, but in Christ Jesus I have no restrictions to all The Blessings that belongs to me.

Chapter 9

HEALING IS YOUR INHERITANCE IN CHRIST

He who dwells in the secret place of the Most High shall remain stable and fixed under the shadow of the Almighty [Whose power no foe can withstand] (Psalm 91:1)

To be truly come out of every unpleasant situations, we must not be too busy to feed our spirit, soul and body with the Word of God. He who dwell in the secret place of the most High shall be protected from all kind of evils. The Lord God prepared the Children of Israel and lead them to the Promised Land. On their way and throughout their journeys, God guided them as to what they needs to do that will make them to truly come out victoriously; He wanted them to be in good health by the time they reached the Promised Land; He doesn't want them broken and battered.

The Word of God promised more blessings to those whose minds stayed on Him (see Isaiah 26:3)

We must not love the world more than The Word of God, the measure we give to the Word of God will determine what we will get from God. I pray that The Lord God will grant us the grace to love and embrace His Words in The Name of Jesus Christ.

To enjoy the healing and health God planned for us to have, we must not be sin or poverty conscious, we must be more of God's Word conscious. We must give more attention to the Word of God and be more healing conscious with The Word of God He gave us in The Bible dwelling in us richly.

God never asked us to be sickness symptoms conscious, He never asked us to be the medical science words conscious, God wants our attentions. He wants us to be full of Him, not to be full of our symptoms, feelings, nor our challenges. He want us to start thinking and says what He says not what satan wants us to say and not what our symptoms tries to dictate to us.

To Be out of bondages, we must Be More of God's Word conscious and not sickness conscious.

The word of God must dwell in us richly enough to flush away from us every wrong thinking's.

Resist the devil, it will flee from you is what the Bible says, we must not dwell on the symptoms of sickness, and we must not dwell on any wrong feelings, but rather to dwell on the Word of God, to meditate on the Word of God, to ponder over it. As we give more attentions to the Father God's Word as it is in the Bible, God will only give us healing and not sickness.

God desired the Children of Israel to be well on their way to the Promised Land, He advised them on the types of foods they should eat and what they should not eat. He advised them to fast to discipline their flesh, He advised them to have control over their flesh and their eating habits (Leviticus 16:29, 1 Cor. 6:13)

> It shall be a statute to you forever that in the seventh month [nearly October] on the tenth day of the month you shall afflict yourselves [by fasting with penitence and humiliation] and do no work at all, either the native-born or the stranger who dwells temporarily among you. For on this day atonement shall be made for you, to cleanse you; from all your sins you shall be clean before the Lord. It is a Sabbath of [solemn] rest to you, and you shall afflict yourselves [by fasting with penitence and humiliation]; it is a statute forever (Leviticus 16: 29-31)

Though God advised the Israelites to fast in the tenth day of the seventh month, Christians should fast and pray as God leads them always and God will give a Sabbath of rest from any activities that is not profitable to us and He will save us from every activities that does not bring glory to The Name of The Lord. He will prepared us and save us from anything that is trying to distract us from enjoying God's best for us. Therefore, it does not mean being idle doing nothing, it means being able to slow down to hear God's best directions for us, and as soon as we hear Him, we should follow the directions. I pray that we will be able to hear God and obey in The Name of Jesus Christ, I pray that God will grant us the Wisdom, the Spirit of understanding, the finances, the energy and the time to study His Words.

Scriptures on Healing

Saying, If you will diligently hearken to the voice of the Lord your God and will do what is right in His sight, and will listen to and obey His commandments and keep all His statutes, I will put none of the diseases upon you which I brought upon the Egyptians, for I am the Lord Who heals you (Exodus 15:26)

Bless (affectionately, gratefully praise) the Lord, O my soul; and all that is [deepest] within me, bless His holy name! Bless (affectionately, gratefully praise) the Lord, O my soul, and forget not [one of] all His benefits— Who forgives [every one of] all your iniquities, Who heals [each one of] all your diseases. Who redeems your life from the pit and corruption, Who beautifies, dignifies, and crowns you with loving-kindness and tender mercy. Who satisfies your mouth [your necessity and desire at your personal age and situation] with good so that your youth, renewed, is like the eagle's [strong, overcoming, soaring]! (Psalm 103: 1-5)

Surely He has borne our griefs (sicknesses, weaknesses, and distresses) and carried our sorrows and pains [of punishment], yet we [ignorantly] considered Him stricken, smitten, and afflicted by God [as if with leprosy]. But He was wounded for our transgressions, He was bruised for our guilt and iniquities; the chastisement [needful to obtain] peace and well-being for us was upon Him, and with the stripes [that wounded] Him we are healed and made whole (Isaiah 53: 4-5)

So the report of Him spread throughout all Syria, and they brought Him all who were sick, those afflicted with various diseases and torments, those under the power of demons, and epileptics, and paralyzed people, and He healed them (Matthew 4:24)

When evening came, they brought to Him many who were under the power of demons, and He drove out the spirits with a word and restored to health all who were sick. And thus He fulfilled what was spoken by the prophet Isaiah, He Himself took [in order to carry away] our weaknesses and infirmities and bore away our diseases (Matthew 8: 16-17)

Jesus turned around and, seeing her, He said, Take courage, daughter! Your faith has made you well. And at once the woman was restored to health (Matthew 9:22)

And Jesus, in pity, touched their eyes; and instantly they received their sight and followed Him (Matthew 20:34)

And the blind and the lame came to Him in the porches and courts of the temple, and He cured them (Matthew 21:14)

For He had healed so many that all who had distressing bodily diseases kept falling upon Him and pressing upon Him in order that they might touch Him (Mark 3: 10)

For Jesus was commanding, Come out of the man, you unclean spirit! (Mark 5:8)

And they came to Jesus and looked intently and searchingly at the man who had been a demoniac, sitting there, clothed and in his right mind, [the same man] who had had the legion [of demons]; and they were seized with alarm and struck with fear (Mark 5:15)

And He said to her, Daughter, your faith (your trust and confidence in Me, springing from faith in God) has restored you to health. Go in (into) peace and be continually healed and freed from your [distressing bodily] disease (Mark 5:34)

And when He had gone in, He said to them, why do you make an uproar and weep? The little girl is not dead but is sleeping (Mark 5:39)

Gripping her [firmly] by the hand, He said to her, Talitha cumi—which translated is, Little girl, I say to you, arise [from the sleep of death]! And instantly the girl got up and started walking around—for she was twelve years old. And they were utterly astonished and overcome with amazement. And He strictly commanded and warned them that no one should know this, and He [expressly] told them to give her [something] to eat (Mark 5: 41-43)

And He called to Him the Twelve [apostles] and began to send them out [as His ambassadors] two by two and gave them authority and power over the unclean spirits (Mark 6:7)

And wherever He came into villages or cities or the country, they would lay the sick in the marketplaces and beg Him that they might touch even the fringe of His outer garment, **and as many as touched Him were restored to health** (Mark 6: 56)

And He said to her, Because of this saying, you may go your way; the demon has gone out of your daughter [permanently]. And she went home and found the child thrown on the couch, and the demon departed (Mark 7: 29-30)

And they were overwhelmingly astonished, saying, He has done everything excellently (commendably and nobly)! He even makes the deaf to hear and the dumb to speak!
(Mark 7:37)

And God did unusual and extraordinary miracles by the hands of Paul. So that handkerchiefs or towels or aprons which had touched his skin were carried away and put upon the sick, and their diseases left them and the evil spirits came out of them (Acts 19: 11-12)

In conclusion, be strong in the Lord [**be empowered through your union with Him**]; draw your strength from Him [that strength which His boundless might provides]. Put on God's whole armour [the armour of a heavy-armed soldier which God supplies], that you may be able successfully to stand up against [all] the strategies and the deceits of the devil. For we are not wrestling with flesh and blood [contending only with physical opponents], but against the despotisms, against the powers, against [the master spirits who are] the world rulers of this present darkness, against the spirit forces of wickedness in the heavenly (supernatural) sphere (Ephesians 6:10-12)

For this is the covenant that I will make with the house of Israel after those days, says the Lord: I will imprint My laws upon their minds, even upon their innermost thoughts and understanding, and engrave them upon their hearts; and I will be their God, and they shall be My people (Hebrews 8:10)

He personally bore our sins in His [own] body on the tree [as on an altar and offered
Himself on it], that we might die (cease to exist) to sin and live to righteousness. By His wounds you have been healed (1 Peter 2:24)

Chapter 10

GOD DELIGHTS IN OUR PROSPERITY

Beloved, I pray that you may prosper in every way
and [that your body] may keep well, even as [I
know] your soul keeps well and prospers (3 John
1:2)

Our prosperities pleases God, God wants us to enjoy life,
to have life and enjoy it in abundance, that is one the
reason why Jesus came to save us. He did not come to
save us and then leave us in abject poverty, if anyone is
not living above the standard blessings set by God The
Almighty, then they should pray and ask God to empower
them to start doing so.

For us to be truly prosperous, our souls must prospers in
The Word of God, we must make the sacrifice of setting
time apart to study the Word of God concerning all things,
especially on how to manage our resources well. To be

truly prosperous, we must prosper in all things; we must prosper in our relationship with God and with man. If we lack what it takes to build a good God glorifying relationships that endure (last) we should pray to God to empower us with the ability to do so.

Choosing to study The Word of God on all subjects and topics is the quickest route to learn the will of God and form the habit to abide with them. From Genesis to Revelations, God emphasises that He delights in the prosperity of His Children. Gods Promise to bless us is certain: Gods prosperity plans for us is certain. God's plan to bless us is certain, they are yes and amen.

Christ is Not Poor

> And as He was praying, the appearance of His countenance became altered (different), and His raiment became dazzling white [flashing with the brilliance of lightning]. And behold, two men were conversing with Him—Moses and Elijah,
> Who appeared in splendour and majesty and brightness ………..
> (Luke 9: 29-31)

Splendour, Majesty and Brightness is not a sign of poverty, but a sign of wealth. God wants His Children to manifest His Blessings and wealth everywhere they go. He wants the world to see that we are truly blessed and not curse. I pray that all our actions will lead us to manifest God's Blessings and not poverty and lack in The Name of Jesus Christ.

Think Big It Pleases God (and God did not rebuke their daring)

> And they saw the God of Israel [that is, a convincing manifestation of His presence], and under His feet it was like pavement of bright sapphire stone, like the very heavens in clearness. And upon the nobles of the Israelites He laid not His hand [to conceal Himself from them, to rebuke their daring, or to harm them]; but they saw [the manifestation of the presence of] God, and ate and drank (Exodus 24:10-11)

In your attempt to come out of bondage, men may try to rebuke you, but God will not rebuke you. The brother of David tried to rebuke him for his daring to come forward to fight the Goliath, to attempt something great for God but God gave him the grace to withstand them, God gave him the grace to ignore them (1 Samuel 17: 26-37) The Bible advices that we should not be afraid of their faces:

> Before I formed you in the womb I knew [and] approved of you [as My chosen instrument], and before you were born I separated and set you apart, consecrating you; [and] I appointed you as a prophet to the nations. Then said I, Ah, Lord God!

Behold, I cannot speak, for I am only a youth. But the Lord said to me, Say not, I am only a youth; for you shall go to all to whom I shall send you, and whatever I command you, you shall speak. Be not afraid of them [their faces], for I am with you to deliver you, says the Lord (Jeremiah 1: 5-8)

Victory in Christ Jesus

No weapon formed against you to stop you from rising, to stop you from achieving your God's given purpose shall prosper in The Name of Jesus Christ. If anyone or anything tries to rebuke you while you are trying to achieve your God's given purpose, the rebuke shall not prosper in The Name of Jesus Christ.

Scriptures That Reminds Us That God Delights in Our Prosperity

Then the Lord said to Moses, Behold, I will rain bread from the heavens for you; and the people shall go out and gather a day's portion every day. That I may prove them, whether they will walk in My law or not (Exodus 16:4)

So Moses and Aaron said to all Israel, at evening **you shall know** that the Lord has brought you out from the land of Egypt (Exodus 16:6)

And when the dew had gone, behold, upon the face of the wilderness there lay a fine, round and flakelike thing, as fine as hoarfrost on the ground (Exodus 16:14)

And Moses said, this is the thing which the Lord commanded you to do, and the glory of the Lord will appear to you....... Moses and Aaron went into the Tent of Meeting, and when they came out they blessed the people, and the glory of the
Lord [the Shekinah cloud] appeared to all the people [as promised] (Leviticus 9:6, 23)

But you shall [earnestly] remember the Lord your God, for it is He Who gives you power to get wealth, that He may establish His covenant which He swore to your fathers, as it is this day (Deuteronomy 8:18)

For the land which you go in to possess is not like the land of Egypt, from which you came out, where you sowed your seed and watered it with your foot laboriously as in a garden of vegetables. But the land which you enter to possess is a land of hills and valleys which drinks water of the rain of the heavens. A land for which the Lord your God cares; the eyes of the Lord your God are always upon it from the beginning of the year to the end of the year. And if you will diligently heed My commandments which I command you this day—to love the Lord your God and to serve Him with all your [mind and] heart and with your entire being— I will give the rain for your land in its season, the early rain and the latter rain, that you may gather in your grain, your new wine, and your oil. And I will give grass in your fields for your cattle that you may eat and be full. (Deuteronomy 11:10-15)

God is not a man that He should tell or act a lie, neither the son of man, that He should feel repentance or compunction [for what He has promised]. Has He said and shall He not do it? Or has He spoken and shall He not make it good? You see, I have received His command to bless Israel. He has blessed, and I cannot reverse or qualify it. (Numbers 23: 19-20)

If you will listen diligently to the voice of the Lord your God, being watchful to do all His commandments which I command you this day, the Lord your God will set you high above all the nations of the earth. And all these blessings shall come upon you and overtake you if you heed the voice of the Lord your God. Blessed shall you be in the city and blessed shall you be in the field. Blessed shall be the fruit of your body and the fruit of your ground and the fruit of your beasts, the increase of your cattle and the young of your flock. Blessed shall be your basket and your kneading trough. Blessed shall you be when you come in and blessed shall you be when you go out. The Lord shall cause your enemies who rise up against you to be defeated before your face; they shall come out against you one way and flee before you seven ways. The Lord shall command the blessing upon you in your storehouse and in all that you undertake. And He will bless you in the land which the Lord your God gives you. The Lord will establish you as a people holy to Himself, as He has sworn to you, if you keep the commandments of the Lord your God and walk in His ways. And all people of the earth shall see that you are called by the name [and in the presence of] the Lord, and they shall be afraid of you. And the Lord shall make you have a surplus of prosperity, through the fruit of your body, of your livestock, and of your ground, in the land which the Lord swore to your fathers to give you. The Lord shall open to you His good treasury, the heavens, to give the rain of your land in its season and to bless all the work of your hands; and you shall lend to many nations, but you shall not borrow. And the Lord shall make you the head, and not the tail; and you shall be above only, and you shall not be beneath, if you heed the commandments of the Lord your God which I command you this day and are watchful to do them. And you shall not turn aside from any of the words which I command you this day, to the right hand or to the left, to go after other gods to serve them. (Deuteronomy 28:1-14)

God is not a man that He should tell or act a lie, neither the son of man, that He should feel repentance or compunction [for what He has promised]. Has He said and shall He not do it? Or has He spoken and shall He not make it good? You see, I have received His command to bless Israel. He has blessed, and I cannot reverse or qualify it. **[God] has not beheld iniquity in Jacob [for he is forgiven],** neither has He seen mischief or perverseness in Israel [for the same reason]. The Lord their God is with Israel, and the shout of praise to their King is among the people. God brought them forth out of Egypt; they have as it were the strength of a wild ox. Surely there is no enchantment with or against Jacob, neither is there any divination with or against Israel. [In due season and even] now it shall be said of Jacob and of Israel, What has God wrought! (Numbers 23:19-23)

Hannah said, let your handmaid find grace in your sight. So [she] went her way and ate, **her countenance no longer sad.** The family rose early the next morning, worshiped before the Lord, and returned to their home in Ramah. Elkanah knew Hannah his wife, and the Lord remembered her (1 Samuel 1:18-19)

.........on the fourteenth day they rested and made it a day of feasting and gladness. But the Jews who were in Shushan [Susa] assembled on the thirteenth day and on the fourteenth, and on the fifteenth day they rested and made it a day of feasting and gladness. Therefore the Jews of the villages, who dwell in the unwalled towns, make the fourteenth day of the month of Adar a day of gladness and feasting, a holiday, and a day for sending choice portions to one another(Esther 9: 17-19)

Blessed (happy, fortunate, prosperous, and enviable) is the man who walks and lives not in the counsel of the ungodly [following their advice, their plans and purposes], nor stands [submissive and inactive] in the path where sinners walk, nor sits down [to relax and rest] where the scornful [and the mockers] gather. But his delight and desire are in the law of the Lord, and on His law (the precepts, the instructions, the teachings of God) he habitually meditates (ponders and studies) by day and by night. And he shall be like a tree firmly planted [and tended] by the streams of water, ready to bring forth its fruit in its season; its leaf also shall not fade or wither; and everything he does shall prosper [and come to maturity] (Psalms 1: 1-3)

Sing, O barren one, you who did not bear; break forth into singing and cry aloud, you who did not travail with child! For the [spiritual] children of the desolate one will be more than the children of the married wife, says the Lord. Enlarge the place of your tent, and let the curtains of your habitations be stretched out; spare not; lengthen your cords and strengthen your stakes. For you will spread abroad to the right hand and to the left; and your offspring will possess the nations and make the desolate cities to be inhabited. Fear not, for you shall not be ashamed; neither be confounded and depressed, for you shall not be put to shame. For you shall forget the shame of your youth, and you shall not [seriously] remember the reproach of your widowhood any more (Isaiah 54:1-4)

You afflicted [city], storm-tossed and not comforted, behold, I will set your stones in fair colours [in antimony to enhance their brilliance] and lay your foundations with sapphires. And I will make your windows and pinnacles of [sparkling] agates or rubies, and your gates of [shining] carbuncles, and all your walls [of your enclosures] of precious stones (Isaiah 54:11-12)

But He replied to them, Give them something to eat yourselves. And they said to Him, Shall we go and buy 200 denarii [about forty dollars] worth of bread and give it to them to eat? And He said to them, how many loaves do you have? Go and see. And when they [had looked and] knew, they said, Five [loaves] and two fish (Mark 6:37-38)

Then He commanded the people all to recline on the green grass by companies (Mark 6:39)

And taking the five loaves and two fish, He looked up to heaven and, praising God, gave thanks and broke the loaves and kept on giving them to the disciples to set before the people; and He [also] divided the two fish among [them] all (Mark 6:41)

And they all ate and were satisfied (Mark 6:42)

And He went up into the boat with them, and the wind ceased (sank to rest as if exhausted by its own beating). And they were astonished exceedingly [beyond measure] (Mark 6:51)

....................and as many as touched Him were restored to health (Mark 6: 56)

And He said to her, Because of this saying, you may go your way; the demon has gone out of your daughter [permanently]. And she went home and found the child thrown on the couch, and the demon departed (Mark 7: 29-30)

And they were overwhelmingly astonished, saying, He has done everything excellently (commendably and nobly)! He even makes the deaf to hear and the dumb to speak! (Mark 7:37)

Breaking the power of the spirit of idleness.....whoever desires to be great among you must be your servant. And whoever wishes to be most important and first in rank among you must be slave of all (Mark 10:43-44)

And her neighbours and relatives heard that the Lord had shown great mercy on her, and they rejoiced with her (Luke 1:58)

Blessed (praised and extolled and thanked) be the Lord, the God of Israel, because He has come and brought deliverance and redemption to His people! And He has raised up a Horn of salvation [a mighty and valiant Helper, the Author of salvation] for us in the house of David His servant— This is as He promised by the mouth of His holy prophets from the most ancient times [in the memory of man]— That we should have deliverance and be saved from our enemies and from the hand of all who detest and pursue us with hatred. To make true and show the mercy and compassion and kindness [promised] to our forefathers and to remember and carry out His holy covenant [to bless, which is all the more sacred because it is made by God Himself]. That covenant He sealed by oath to our forefather Abraham: To grant us that we, being delivered from the hand of our foes, might serve Him fearlessly. (Luke 1: 68-74)

And as He was praying, the appearance of His countenance became altered (different), and His raiment became dazzling white [flashing with the brilliance of lightning]. And behold, two men were conversing with Him—Moses and Elijah, Who appeared in splendour and majesty and brightness ……….. (Luke 9: 29-31)

However I tell you truly, there are some of those standing here who will not taste death before they see the kingdom of God. Now about eight days after these teachings, Jesus took with Him Peter and John and James and went up on the mountain to pray. And as He was praying, the appearance of His countenance became altered (different), and His raiment became dazzling white [flashing with the brilliance of lightning]. And behold, two men were conversing with Him— Moses and Elijah, Who appeared in splendour and majesty and brightness and were speaking of His exit [from life], which He was about to bring to realization at Jerusalem. Now Peter and those with him were weighed down with sleep, but when they fully awoke, they saw His glory (splendour and majesty and brightness) and the two men who stood with Him (Luke 9: 27-32)

And they have overcome (conquered) him by means of the blood of the Lamb and by the utterance of their testimony…. (Revelation 12:11)

BECOMING A CHRISTIAN

Becoming a Christian is not a difficult task at all. The Holy Bible instructs every mankind to be born again by confessing our sin and accept Jesus Christ as our Lord and Saviour by praying a simple prayer of salvation.

Prayer of Salvation

Father God, I come to You in the Name of Jesus Christ. According to your Word in the book of Roman 10:9, which says "If you acknowledge and confess with your lips that Jesus is Lord and in your heart believe (adhere to, trusts in, and rely on the truth) that God raised Him from the dead, you will be saved.
I confess Jesus Christ as my Lord and Saviour, Lord Jesus come into my life and forgive me for all my sins. Be Lord of my life in Jesus name, Amen.

Congratulations if you have just prayed this prayer, you are now a Christian and you are saved.

You now have rights to all the promises of God in the Holy Bible.

I will advise you to read the Holy Bible and other Christian literatures regularly to build up your faith in the Lord. Also you will need a Word based church to attend regularly.

Be part of a good local church that teaches Christian to grow in The Word of God.

*****Please write to us to inform us of your new decision you made to become a Christian and we will continue to offer all helps necessary for you to grow in Christ.**

Remain Blessed

Yours in Christ

Folake Hassan (Mrs)

Founder/President: The Blessed Christian Centre

ABOUT THE AUTHOR

Folake Hassan is the Author of the book titled The Attributes of God. She is the Owner of The Online Christian Bookshop named The Blessed Christian: www.theblessedchristian.co.uk . It is Folake's passion to see souls saved and confess Jesus Christ as their Lord and Saviour. Folake Hassan is blessed with 3 children with the youngest being 18 years of age at the time of writing this book. Folake and her children live in London, United Kingdom

About The Book

Coming Out of Bondage is a book written to encourage and inspire someone to desire the best lifestyle God purposed for them. It is to show someone **that no situation is hopeless**, people can come out of every unpleasant situations with the help of the Holy Spirit. People will study in this book the simple practical steps to take to be truly free to enjoy the abundant life God purposed for them.

www.ingramcontent.com/pod-product-compliance
Lightning Source LLC
Chambersburg PA
CBHW021005090426
42738CB00007B/663